Amazing Grace for Survivors

Amazing Grace for Survivors

50 Stories of Faith, Hope, & Perseverance

Edited by
Jeff Cavins, Matthew Pinto,
Patti Maguire Armstrong, and Luke Armstrong

West Chester, Pennsylvania

Ascension Press
Post Office Box 1990
West Chester, PA 19380
Orders: 1-800-376-0520
www.AscensionPress.com

Cover design: Devin Schadt

Printed in the United States of America
08 09 10 11 7 6 5 4 3 2 1

ISBN 978-1-934217-47-4

*To all survivors who have persevered in hope
and grown in faith through God's amazing grace.*

*— Jeff Cavins, Matthew Pinto,
Patti Maguire Armstrong, and Luke Armstrong*

Contents

Introduction... *1*

Chapter 1 – Expect the Unexpected

Extra Innings
Hal McCoy...*3*

Deliver Us from Bullies
Nellie Edwards..*8*

Homeless in Rome
Pat Sagsveen *11*

He Opened the Door to Our Hearts
Connie Goss *15*

Divine Images
Jason Jenicke..*20*

Providential Cookies and Rent
Anita Usher..*25*

Everyday Hero
Chet Czubko, Jr....*29*

Chapter 2 – With God All Things Are Possible

The Road to the Rebels
Immaculée Ilibagiza..*35*

Lion! Oh My!
Peggy M. Podboy *42*

Safe Harbor
Luke Armstrong *46*

All the World's a Stage
Father Benjamin Francis *50*

Loving the Rapist's Child
Heather Gemmen Wilson *62*

One in Faith
Rebecca Lengenfelder *66*

Chapter 3 – He Picked Me Up When I Was Down

All Is Forgiven, Sadie Hawkins!
Mark P. Shea *73*

Survivors' Wisdom (quotations)
Various *76*

Marriage Marathon
Luke Armstrong *80*

Mary, the Mother Who Waits – Part One
Heidi Hess Saxton *85*

Stay and Be Light
Mark Mallett *88*

Bald and Beautiful
Marybeth Hicks *94*

Chapter 4 – The Lighter Side of Surviving

The Incense That Burned My Pride Away
Matt Fern *99*

G.P.S. S.O.S. – *cartoon*
George Abbott *103*

Surviving Kid Country
Tim Bete *104*

A Wheel Dilemma – *cartoon*
George Abbott *106*

Survivors' Humor
Various *107*

Survivor: Suburbia – *cartoon*
George Abbott *109*

Surviving *Survivor*
Tim Bete *110*

Bounced by Bureaucracy – *cartoon*
George Abbott *112*

The Scales of Injustice
Elizabeth Schmeidler *113*

Survivors' One-Liners
Anonymous *116*

Chapter 5 – His Healing Touch

Never Say Never
Susan Brinkmann *119*

Battling with Pregnancy
Ashli McCall *124*

A Doctor *and* a Catholic
Laura Archuleta *128*

The Gift of Cancer
Susan Brinkmann *135*

Against All Odds
Michael Jordan Segal *139*

The Most Glorious Vocation
Susan Babcock *145*

Chapter 6 – Family Matters

The "Imperfect" Storm
Jim Cantore. *149*

Blessed and Broken
Cathy Adamkiewicz *153*

Just Come Home
Margaret Williams *161*

God Hears a Mother's Prayers
Susan Brinkmann. *168*

Full Circle
Chuck Piola *172*

In His Hands
Elizabeth Matthews *177*

Triple Blessing
Melody LaFountain *182*

Chapter 7 – Life Is Precious

Melissa
Patricia M. Devlin *187*

Survival of the Human Spirit
Luke Armstrong *190*

A Former Altar Boy on Death Row
Luke Armstrong *193*

Don't Jump
John Gallagher *199*

Steadfast Love
Nancy Patin Falini 207

Survival Day-by-Day
Chris Cash 213

The Baby Who Would Not Die
As told to Rob L. Staples 216

৵

Acknowledgments 219

Editor and Contributor Contact Information. 221

About the Editors. 223

Introduction

For when I am weak, then I am strong.
— 2 Cor 12:10

Surviving is more than just getting through an ordeal. It is being triumphant in spirit, regardless of the outcome. As Christians, we recognize that life's struggles can bring us strength and peace—even if the struggles remain. Such challenges are the fire that purifies and empowers us, "just as gold and silver are refined and purified by fire" (Zech 13:9). When trouble comes our way, our faith may be tested, but our endurance grows and our character is strengthened.

This is a message that we, in our human weakness, often run from. "Suffering? Please no!" We may be tempted to question our faith—and even the existence of God—due to the suffering we witness in the world and experience in our own lives. Yet, when confronted with the inevitable hardships of this world, we can be fortified if we move forward steeled by God's grace. Though the flesh is indeed weak, the spirit can overcome.

As the inspiring stories in this book attest, suffering is never the end but the means—to deeper union with God and peace within. For many whose trials are chronicled in these pages, initial anger and rebellion gave way to a profound peace and purpose by the grace of acceptance. By the end of his or her particular trial, each emerged stronger than when he or she began. This is the very definition of survival.

Friendship with God does not spare us difficulties. Rather,

it is through these difficulties that we can truly come to know Him and experience His loving providence in our lives. As Our Lord told St. Paul, "My grace is sufficient for you, for my power is made perfect in weakness" (2 Cor 12:9).

As long as we live, we will know pain. But God's own Son experienced suffering and death, so we know that power is hidden in pain. Jesus' suffering, though, was not the end of the story; the resurrection was still to come. If we unite our crosses with the cross of Christ, we will receive the redemptive graces that lead to the resurrection. We will find peace and joy and arise triumphant.

The experiences of those in this book are a testimony to God's power as He forms and strengthens us through His grace. We will experience the pain of these brothers and sisters in faith and share the glory of their triumph. In the end, their grace becomes ours for we are one body in Christ.

– Patti Maguire Armstrong

For all things are for your sakes, so that the grace
which abounds through the many may cause
thanksgiving to abound, to the glory of God.
– 2 Cor 12:10

Chapter 1

Expect the Unexpected

Extra Innings

The first time it happened was an August night in 2000. I was walking up to the press box in St. Louis' Busch Stadium, where the hometown Cardinals were playing the Cincinnati Reds, the baseball team I have covered for the *Dayton Daily News* for the last thirty-one years. Suddenly, everything went blurry in my right eye. I couldn't make out the people next to me. I rubbed my eye, figuring the blurriness would go away.

It didn't. I managed to report the action of that game using just my good eye. But I was worried. I watch baseball games and explain to readers the Reds' performance. To do my job, I have to see everything that happens on the field, from the swagger after a home run hitter's swing to the spin a pitcher puts on his deliveries.

Back home, my wife, Nadine, took me to an ophthalmologist, Dr. Jay Kelman, an old friend of ours. He is always upbeat, but once I got into the chair, he grew quiet. "You've had a stroke of the optic nerve," he finally said. "I'm sending you to a specialist."

"There's good news and bad news," the specialist said after examining me. "The bad news is, the vision in your right eye is never going to get better. The good news is, there's only a fifteen percent chance of it happening in your left eye."

It is amazing how quickly your body adjusts. Almost

immediately, my left eye compensated for the right one. It completely took over. Though I had lost fifty percent of the vision in my right eye, I barely noticed. I went on watching and reporting on ball games, driving my car, playing tennis five days a week. By the end of the season, I had all but forgotten my problem.

Two years passed; good years. My three boys were fine men. Nadine and I were as deeply in love as two people can be. In December 2002, I learned I would be inducted into the writers' wing of the National Baseball Hall of Fame—the highest honor a baseball writer can receive.

In a few weeks, I would be headed to Sarasota, Florida, where the Reds would begin training for the coming season. One morning, I took my time getting up. The only thing on my mind was my morning coffee. Downstairs, Nadine was getting ready for work as a math teacher at a Catholic school. I got to my feet, and everything was dark and fuzzy. I felt my way down the hallway stairs and into the kitchen. Nadine was a blur. I picked up the newspaper sitting on the table. I couldn't read it. "Honey," I said, my voice quivering, "it's here."

"What do you mean?" she asked.

"I got it in my left eye, too." I started sobbing. Nadine tried to console me, but all I could think was, *My career is my life. I can't cover baseball anymore. What am I going to do?*

Nadine drove me straight to the ophthalmologist. My old friend Jay gave it to me straight. "Look," he said. "You have your wife and your sons, and you're in good health otherwise. You're strong enough to handle this, Hal."

I wasn't so sure. We left the doctor's office and headed to the *Daily News*. I had to tell the sports editor, my boss, Frank Corsoe, that I was through. I had worked in that office for most of my adult life. Yet I could hardly manage my way around.

We walked into Frank's office. I handed him the doctor's report. "I'm going to have to retire," I said. I started to say good-bye, but Frank stopped me. "Don't let this thing beat you," he said. "We'll help you. Go down to Sarasota with the team next month. See if you can do it."

How? The next few weeks, my eyesight kept getting worse. I couldn't drive. I called Tony Jackson, the baseball writer for the *Cincinnati Post*—one of my competitors. I told him about my condition and asked if he could chauffeur me from my condo to the games. "Don't feel obligated," I told him.

"You helped me out when I was new to the beat," he said. "I've never forgotten that. I've got you covered."

My first day in Sarasota I went directly to the ballpark. I knew the Reds' clubhouse like the back of my hand. I had covered most of the players for years. I looked around. Now the players were just fuzzy shapes. I stood in the doorway in a daze. Aaron Boone, then the Reds third baseman, came over to me. "What's wrong?" he asked.

"I can't do my job," I said. "I can't see. I have to quit."

Aaron grabbed me by my arm. "I don't want to hear you use the word 'quit' again. You love this job," he said. "What you've told me is not a good enough reason to quit. The guys in this clubhouse will help you any way we can. But you've got to help yourself."

I hardly knew what to say. I agreed to stick it out a few more days. It wasn't easy. I would walk through the clubhouse and knock over a trash can. One day I walked right past a friend I had known for years. At night, I called Nadine and poured out my frustrations. "Things are going to get better. You just have to believe," she assured me.

But they didn't get better. The Reds played day games in Florida. The sun came streaming into the press box. I couldn't see where the ball was hit or the print on my computer screen. One day it took me seven hours to write a story that normally would have taken me only two hours to bang out.

I called my editor. "I want you to promise me something," I said. "If my writing isn't up to snuff, tell me. I don't want to be carried."

"You can do this, Hal," Frank reiterated. He arranged to get me a laptop computer with enlarged type on screen. One of my colleagues, Bob Nightengale, wrote a story about my battle. I started getting e-mail from readers, strangers who said they were praying for me. They begged me not to quit, saying that without my stories, their mornings wouldn't be the same. I can't tell you how those people lifted my spirits, especially their prayers. I thought a lot about those prayers and how much my situation must matter to people if they were willing to pray for me.

But doubt and depression were never far away. Near the end of spring training, I went to Tampa. The Reds had a night game against the New York Yankees. We got there late in the afternoon. I headed toward the clubhouse entrance and felt my way inside. I interviewed some players and then walked onto the field. The late afternoon glare was blinding. A *New York Post* writer, Kevin Kernan, had to lead me upstairs to the press box. I looked at the field. All I could make out were shapes moving around.

I bowed my head. *Help me, Lord. Can I do this anymore? Help me see the truth.* I looked up. The sun set. The glare disappeared, and the stadium lights were on. I couldn't believe it. For the first time since coming to Florida, I could make out the players on the field and the words on my computer screen. Not well, but enough to get by; well enough to do my job. Then it struck me: the Reds play most of their regular-season games at night under these same arc lights. I would soldier through the few games played in bright sunshine. My press box colleagues would help. I grabbed a phone and called Nadine. "I can do this!" I said.

At the end of spring training, the Reds returned to Cincinnati to start the season. My editor arranged for a driver to take me to the ballpark every game. "Your work has been great," Frank said. Sometimes I think my reporting has gotten better. Losing my eyesight has made me a better listener. I am more attuned to what players are feeling and to the subtle rhythms of the game. Early in the season I broke a story about some possible player trades. It was big news.

Last July I was officially inducted into the Hall of Fame. As I stood at the podium, I thought, *Maybe God is showing me there's a purpose in this.* So I told the audience what my setback brought home to me: "Don't ever give up on yourself. Don't ever give up on something you love."

I haven't ever stopped loving Nadine just because I can't see her as well as I used to. Same with baseball. I still get to write about the game, doing what I love most, every single day. How blessed can a man be?

– Hal McCoy

Hal McCoy is a Cincinnati Reds beat writer for the Dayton Daily News. *He was honored by the National Baseball Hall of Fame in 2002 as the winner of the J. G. Taylor Spink Award, which is awarded annually "for meritorious contributions to baseball writing." McCoy has covered the Cincinnati Reds since 1972 and is currently the longest-tenured beat writer for one team in all of Major League Baseball. He has won more than forty writing awards and was the first non-Cincinnati newsperson elected to the Cincinnati Journalists Hall of Fame.*

He is an honors graduate from Kent State University, where he played first base.

Deliver Us from Bullies

Raising a family in a town rife with gang crime was a constant concern for my husband and me. Almost daily there were news stories of drive-by shootings and other assorted acts of violence. In 1994, our town of less than 10,000 people nestled in central Washington state made the national news for having more violent crime per capita than New York City!

We prayed to God that we might be delivered from such an environment, in which our children were not safe to play in the nearby city park. We prayed with more intensity after the police knocked on our door one midnight, telling us, "Lock up tight. We're after a violent gang." It was right behind our home!

After that potentially life-threatening episode, we decided to have our oldest son, John Paul, take tae kwon do in case he would have to protect himself from attack. He was fourteen at the time and loved practicing his new skills on his numerous siblings.

In 1996, God, in His goodness, answered our prayers, and we moved to a small town in the Midwest. We were almost euphoric to live in a place with a population of less than two hundred. After unloading the van, we prayed the Rosary, thanking God for helping us survive the daily threat of harm.

We bought a house right across from a charming park, which years before had seen many more children happily playing on its well-maintained slides, swings, and merry-go-round. Our children would now fill the void, and we had a sense that they were safe to be carefree—just as kids should be.

Independence Day arrived, and it was more relevant than ever for us! Many families in our town welcomed visiting relatives. Among them was a family with some rowdy boys who seemed to take pride in recklessly tearing through every part of town, raising dust and alarm.

With his younger brothers and a few of their friends, John Paul had started a game of basketball while waiting for dusk, when we would have our traditional family fireworks. Suddenly, something whizzed by John Paul's ear, and he turned around to see that a couple of out-of-town boys (about eleven and thirteen years old) were lighting bottle rockets in the center of the park. They were setting them off casually, with no concern that someone might be injured. As we had taught him, John Paul looked out for the younger children, so he approached the boys. He politely asked, "Would you please light your rockets over at the abandoned school grounds?" The boy with the lighter looked at him with a grin and lit the next one, dropping it as before. The speeding projectile miraculously made it through the crowd of kids on the basketball court, so JP (as we sometimes call him) took him by the shoulders and in his words said, "I'm not asking anymore. Move on!" Perhaps since sixteen-year-old John Paul was a head above both boys, they did as they were told, but not without yelling expletives as they ran away.

They called out, "We're going to get our big brother, and he's going to kill you!" Shrugging it off, John Paul went back to the game. In less than five minutes, the same van that had been menacing the town all morning pulled up to the edge of the park. Out climbed three boys, whom our son judged to be between eighteen and twenty years old. The largest strode quickly toward John Paul with fists clenched. He cursed at him for, as he put it, "telling my brother what to do" and slugged John Paul in the face. As he struggled to regain footing, the thought crossed his mind that he could be in tomorrow's headlines—similar to those so common to our former hometown paper.

Just as the other two began to close in on John Paul, he remembered that he knew how to defend himself. Though it had been nearly two years since he had learned tae kwon do, he blocked the next punch and delivered a blow to his aggressor's mouth. Down went the bully, minus a front tooth!

He got back up and made for his van, saying, "I'm going to get my dad!" In just a few minutes, sure enough, came the bully's father. He showed up and demanded that John Paul pay for his son's tooth. John Paul stood his ground and told him that his son had not even asked his side of things before throwing the first punch. The boy's father refused to listen and kept yelling at him to pay up! John Paul just turned and walked away.

We called the sheriff and explained what had transpired. The deputy came and interviewed John Paul. He had already discovered the identity of the others and told us that we should be proud of our son—that he had done well to protect the younger children. The deputy commended him for his heroism. While we encourage our children to follow the Gospel's admonition to "turn the other cheek," the Church does teach that since our bodies are sacred, they are deserving of being defended from aggression.

There will always be bullies; we cannot escape them entirely. But in this case, the bullies we sought to escape in Washington had prepared John Paul for the bullies in our new home, thus proving Romans 8:28: "God can use all things for good for those who love him."

— Nellie Edwards

Nellie Edwards is the mother of eight children. She is a pro-life activist and has built a successful business with her children, replicating her sculpted designs. Last Spring, she realized a talent for fine art painting and has just completed The Light of Life, *depicting Jesus in the womb of his Blessed Mother. Her website is: www.LifeAndTruth.net.*

Homeless in Rome

Surrounded by my friends and classmates in our close-knit group of recent high school graduates, I happily conversed over a glass of wine. In mere months, we would be dispersing across the country, attending a diversity of colleges leading to different lives. But that night, all of our roads led to Rome. We were on our senior trip to the vibrant city that for the past two millennia had held the keys to so much of what we believed.

Amid the enthusiastic conversations going on around me, I reflected contentedly on my day. Our chaperone, Fr. James Shea, was also our teacher, our priest, and our friend. His depth of knowledge added to an already amazing tour of the Vatican, the eternal city built on the ground where our first pope had been laid to rest.

All of us had gone to confession that day, and I was thinking about mine. Rome, like all big cities, has its lion's share of beggars and homeless people. Having grown up in North Dakota, this was not something to which I was accustomed. My reaction towards the homeless surprised me. I resented them. Many were young and seemed capable of working instead of begging. *They are just lazy*, I thought sullenly. "Father," I had confessed, "I just cannot bring myself to feel sorry for them."

Later that evening, as our group prepared to return to our hostel run by nuns, we walked through a political demonstration that transformed the streets into chaos. Keeping a group of twenty-five high school graduates together is difficult in any situation, but it became quite a task in the erupting bedlam. Our chaperones quickly herded us into cabs. Four of my friends stepped into one in front of me. When I tried to join them in the small yellow car, I was told that there was no room. Reluctantly, I entered a cab by myself while Fr. Shea explained in Italian to the driver where to take me.

I watched the city from the cab window as we drove from one

street to another. I was shaken out of my daydream when the cab driver told me to get out in Italian. "What?" I responded. "This isn't right." I had no idea where I was. With the driver's insistent prodding, I disembarked and watched as the cab drove away. I found myself alone and scared. I did not panic, though. I was fairly certain that if I could find my way to the Vatican, I could find my way back to the hostel. Finding the Vatican in Rome would not be difficult.

After about an hour of wandering by foot, I arrived in Saint Peter's Square. In the Square, I saw a man playing a saxophone with a welcoming smile. I explained my situation to him. He was a Norwegian who spoke English. The man told me he was also lost, although I had the impression that he may not have had a place to stay to begin with. I told him that he was welcome to sleep outside the nunnery hostel I was staying at if we could find it. So the two of us set off in the direction I believed would lead us there.

Before long, we arrived at a square I recognized. My hopeful enthusiasm waned, however, after an hour more of walking brought us again to the same square. "You don't know where you are going, do you?" the Norwegian said. He bought me a soda and then went off on his own to find a place to stay.

As I continued to wander, I came to a park. There were three teenage Italian girls there, two of whom spoke English. They offered me a ride, and although I did not know how to get to my hostel, I wanted to go back to the Vatican and try again to walk back. Two of the girls drove me all around the city before they propositioned me. "Are you a ... umm ... are you a gigolo?"

There comes a familiar moment before committing a sin. Here I was, anonymously lost in a big city and was being propositioned by two attractive Italian girls. But I was also in Rome, the seat of my religion. "No," I responded, "I am not a gigolo. Now please take me to the Vatican."

For the third time that day, I was again in Saint Peter's

Square, as lost as ever. The beggars, whom I had looked down upon with disdain hours earlier, still prodded and pleaded for a few coins. The pigeons still fought each other desperately for crumbs of bread, and the people still rushed about everywhere. The Square was still the same as it had been hours earlier, only now I was part of the street life rather than just an onlooker. I gazed up at Saint Peter's Basilica and prayed earnestly to God that I would be found. I reached for my wallet, which contained the emergency numbers to call in case something like this happened, and realized it was gone. I did not know how to get home, and I had no one to call. All I had was a ten-dollar euro note and a pleading prayer: *Christ, I put this in your hands. If you want me to get out of this, please help me.*

With my last ten euros, I took a cab to the American embassy. The Italian police stationed there told me that the next day was the Feast of Saints Peter and Paul, so everything would be closed. Since I did not have contact information for anyone in Rome, the police informed me there was little they could do. I asked if I could at least spend the night there, but they said no. Instead, they recommended that I find a park to sleep in. By now, fatigue and disappointment gave way to fear: *How would I ever reunite with my group?*

I trudged down the street in front of a five-star hotel, where I found a park bench. That would be my bed for the night. As I drifted off into a worried sleep, I thought about my feelings earlier that day regarding the homeless beggars. It occurred to me that some of the people coming in and out of the hotel might be judging me just as harshly as I had judged others. Seeing a young, seemingly capable young man sleeping on a bench might bring forth disdain in them as they stepped into the luxurious hotel for the night. But they did not know my circumstances any more than I knew anyone else's. It was easy to blame them so that I did not have to be compassionate or feel responsible to help in any way. Sometimes bad things happen to good people, and through no fault of their own, they are left destitute. Or maybe they have backgrounds that did not give them the security that I took for granted, having come from a loving home. I prayed for myself that night but also for all those on the streets. While I did not know how I was going to get out of my dilemma, I knew that I would now look with more compassion on others.

The next morning, I walked up to the same embassy entrance and talked to the new Italian guards who had been rotated in. I feared the same answer I had received from the previous set of guards: "There is nothing we can do for you," but with a prayer on my lips, I again approached for their help. I was told that just next door was a United States marine post, staffed twenty-four hours a day. The marines put me in contact with my parents in the United States, who had a number I could call to reach Fr. Shea. My ordeal was finally ended through a phone call to one very relieved chaperone.

My trials in Rome were over, yet I now understood that what had been a traumatic and brief experience for me was a daily struggle for so many. I was homeless in Rome for a night through no fault of my own. I began to suspect that many of those beggars I had judged were not in their predicaments through deliberate choices of their own. Through my night of homelessness, I felt God asking of me: "Now do you understand?"

Yes, I did now understand.

– Pat Sagsveen

Pat Sagsveen is a graduate of St. Mary's High School in Bismarck, North Dakota. He is currently attending the Franciscan University of Steubenville in Ohio. Although Pat is still discerning his future, he is majoring in psychology.

He Opened the Door to Our Hearts

My cousin Pam opened the door to her workplace, the Parker House, a group home for orphaned kids. As we stepped inside, the background hum of children at play filled the air. We carefully sidestepped toys strewn about the floor and, in the kitchen, we found their little owners. About five children around the ages of four or five were busily at play, barely noticing the three intruders: my husband, my son, and me. One boy, quite a bit older than the others, had quickly sat up in a chair and put his hands on his lap as he eyed us eagerly.

"Why aren't you playing?" I asked.

"Oh, I can be good," he responded and jumped from the chair and hugged my husband, Frank. "Hi, I'm PJ," he said.

"I'm Frank," my husband introduced himself warmly, taking the hand that PJ had offered him.

"Did you ever play baseball?" he asked comically, smiling up at my husband.

When we stepped outside, my son, fifteen-year-old Frank Ryan, asked me what that boy was doing there. He continued asking a lot of questions. Then, to my complete surprise, he asked, "Mom, why don't we take him home? Melissa and Mandy have moved out of the house, so we have an extra bedroom."

It was the weekend of the wedding of one of my cousin's nieces. We weren't really close with the family, but since we had been invited, it would be fun to see our relatives in Baton Rouge, Louisiana, for the weekend. Since we were not exactly sure how to get there from our home in Mississippi, we got an early start and ended up arriving with two hours to spare. While we waited for the wedding, we went to visit with my cousin Pam. I had not seen or talked to her in four years. She invited us to see where she worked.

That is how we ended up in the commons area of the Parker House. Pam worked there with the orphan kids who had been left behind. These were the kids that had been in and out of various foster homes but could just not find a home. They were the lost children who had nowhere else to go but the Parker House. PJ had sadly watched as his brother and sister had been adopted but not him. Since the age of five, the poor little boy was slapped with the crushing reality: nobody wants me. Most of the other kids at the Parker Houses were between the ages and four and six. PJ, at eleven, was the oldest child there. It seemed unlikely that he would ever find a family of his own.

As we left the Parker House and the scenery rushed by the window on the way back to the wedding, a contemplative silence filled our van. We were all thinking about PJ. I just could not get his eager face and smile out of my mind—the way he had sought out my husband and connected with him; the way his pleading eyes had looked up at all of us. Pam later told me that it was very rare for him to connect with adult males as he had done instantly with Frank. "Mom, don't forget about him," my son said to me as we arrived at the wedding.

At the wedding, most of the conversations had revolved around PJ and the Parker House. As I talked to everyone about the kids there, another cousin injected some reality into the situation. She had a son with disabilities, so she spoke from experience. She explained that all these kids had their lion's share of issues. Anyone considering taking in an orphan needed to be realistic about what to expect. She and her husband had once considered adopting one of these kids, but because their own son had disabilities, they felt it would be too much for them to take on.

"But PJ looks like just an ordinary kid," I told her, remembering how normal he had appeared.

"Oh, they may look like normal kids, Connie, but they are not," she continued. "They have been passed around from foster home to foster home. These are the kids that no one wants. Some of them start fires, commit crimes, and cause real damage to 'normal' families."

I knew that PJ needed something more than what he had; I just was not sure if we had enough of what he needed to give to him. It broke my heart to think of him without a father or mother connection. Knowing he must be deeply wounded inside, yet strong enough to try and win us over, I was captivated by him.

In spite of my doubts, PJ seemed God sent. Even though I had no idea even where to begin to adopt a child, something inside me told me that this was meant to be. The morning after we returned from the wedding, I started asking the questions I needed to: *What can we do? Who can we call? Where do we even start?* I was determined to do what needed to be done to make PJ a part of our family.

I got in touch with various foundations and establishments. Often, I was told to call this place or that, only to be directed to still another place. I was put in touch with the Harding House of Jackson, Mississippi, and the staff there helped me through the many steps that are involved in adopting, such as home-licensing and interviews to make sure that our family could provide a stable environment. During the next month, my mind was a whirl of thoughts that centered on PJ. Forgetting him was not an option for me. I thought about him all the time. "Mom, don't forget about PJ. We have an extra room here," my son would often say to me.

If the paperwork or rules seemed overwhelming to me, my husband would say: "Just get back on the phone. He's meant to be with us." Frank had been touched by the way PJ had gone right up to him that day we met him. He wanted to be PJ's father.

My coworkers thought I was crazy. "You don't know what you are getting into," they would tell me. While we did not know exactly what we were doing, or how we were going to do it, we knew that this was right, that God had put PJ directly into our path. We were determined to do whatever it took to give him a loving home, and we prayed with conviction that this would happen.

There were classes to go to, certifications to obtain, and

countless forms to be filled out. The process was tedious and more complicated because it would be an out-of-state adoption. At one point, Frank and I were offered the opportunity to consider the many children available for adoption in our own state. "You don't understand," I told them. "I met him; he's in my heart. We were not looking. This was meant to be."

Unfortunately, the months dragged on as we worked our way through all the red tape. If my son saw the box of paperwork put away on my closet shelf, he would take it down and put it on the kitchen table. "Momma, you promised you wouldn't forget PJ," Frank Ryan would remind me. It took two years before we got visitation rights to see PJ again. We did not want to get his hopes up, so he did not know that there was a family in the next state working tirelessly to give him the love that he deserved. We sent him a big stuffed dog at Christmas, but the card had to say it was Santa and not from us. No one wanted to get his hopes up in case it did not work out for some reason.

Our daughter, who was attending beauty school at the time, came with us when we were able to visit PJ two years after we had first met him. Our hearts raced in anticipation as we drove back to Baton Rouge. *Would he remember us? Would he like us? Would this work out?* We checked into a hotel and anxiously made our way to the Parker House. My husband was nervous about walking into the house again because he knew that he would want to adopt more than just PJ when he saw the other abandoned kids. When we walked in, the kids were all engrossed with playing video games.

There was PJ, with a controller in hand. When he saw us, he put the controller down and came up to us. "I know how to clean," he said, "and I know how to sweep. I'm a good boy." The kids are trained to see any visitor as a potential parent, and they are eager to please in the hopes of finding a home. When he came up to us like that, it brought tears to our eyes. This young boy, who we had been working tirelessly to bring into our family, still desperately wanted a loving home. For us, there could be no leaving him. We adopted PJ and made him a part of our family.

PJ had been at the Parker House for five years. So much of his precious youth was spent not belonging to anyone. He had all but given up hope of ever finding a family. When he first came into our home, he took everything out of our cabinets and reorganized them, to show us that he could clean and be a "good boy." It was not always an easy adjustment for PJ, and we worked lovingly to help erase the effects of his troubled past. He came to us on eight different medications. From nightmares to anxiety to his ADHD, he was constantly medicated for a laundry list of ailments.

It would break my heart when he would be disciplined for something and he would go to his room and pack his suitcase. At any minor infraction he would think that we were going to send him back to the Parker House. I had to hide the suitcases from him! "We're not going to send you home, honey," I would tell him. "This is your house, your room, and we are your family now."

In the four years since he came to live with us, PJ has improved by leaps and bounds. He was slowly weaned off all but one of his prescriptions. PJ has come to believe that this is not a temporary thing; he is here for good, and we love him. We had never thought about adopting and we did not know anything about it. We learned that it does not have to take much money, only patience and time. PJ is a survivor. He survived heartache and abandonment, yet he still kept trying to succeed at finding a family of his own. Finally, he did. Through PJ and the grace of God, our capacity to love has grown, and we have been greatly blessed by a very special son.

– Connie Goss

Connie Goss is employed as a lab technician. She is married to Frank, a police lieutenant, whom she says is an extraordinary husband and father. They have two beautiful grandchildren, Michael Ryan, five, and Riley Clark, two.

Divine Images

Looking into the eyes beneath my paint brush, I held my breath. Each stroke had to be just right. You see, I was looking into the face of Jesus—one I created on canvas with oils.

Hours ticked by like minutes as I became completely lost in my work. I did not want this picture to be just beautiful; I wanted it to be real. As real as the Jesus who touched my life, pulled me out of despair, and set me on a path I never expected as a religious artist.

When making my paintings, I feel the gratitude of one saved from a life of desperation and placed on a path laid out by God. So now, all I can do is spend my life loving Him through the gift of art He has given me.

When I entered the University of Kansas to major in fine arts, it was with the enthusiastic expectation one feels just prior to a big adventure. I was ready to spread my wings. I loved my parents and four siblings, but the carefree feeling of being on my own left me buoyant. My only real responsibility would be to show up at class, and I often did not even do that.

Everything was up to me now—who I spent time with, where I went, what I did. As I look back, it was all about *me* then. Nothing else really mattered, not even God. Although I came from a strong, church-going family, skipping church on Sundays became easier with practice. My conscience was shouted down by my supposed higher level thinking, which determined that Christ was really not God's Son. I concluded that He was a mere man conjured into a divine folk hero by wishful thinkers and deceptive historians. I had no need for a religion that laid restrictive, archaic values on the ignorant.

I hid these thoughts from my parents. I loved them and did not want to inflict the pain on them that I disdained their Catholic faith as outdated and simple-minded. I did what I wanted in an amoral atmosphere. There were plenty of friends and parties. Lots of laughs. No rules. And no God.

As the years passed—from my freshman to sophomore to junior year—the fast lane that once pulled me in began pulling me down. It was not fun any more. Still, I could not stop. I was in a fog—thick and dull headed, too lazy to move but too unmotivated to change things. I often slept through the classes for which I bothered to show up. The only thing that lifted me above total irresponsibility was my art. I still cared enough about art to put forth an effort.

It was during my junior year that on old friend from high school called me to inquire about a website he had heard of on near-death experiences. I was intrigued. "Near death experiences? Sounds cool," I said.

Curiosity led me to the site. It was full of stories from people who were near death—and even clinically dead—before resuscitation. In story after story, people told of encountering Jesus, a loving, gentle God. It was not what I expected, but it was what I so desperately needed; a reason to believe again. For the first time in many years, I felt a push toward God and away from darkness.

My conversion began gradually. "Maybe there is something to this after all," I admitted. I started going to church again at the Saint Lawrence Catholic Campus Center. In the beginning, I was not going every Sunday, but at least when I did not go, I felt like I had missed something.

My older brother Jeremy went to the same university and was involved at the center. He encouraged me to attend an upcoming Catholic conference for young adults. *A conference full of religious people,* I thought. *No thanks.* Jeremy was persistent, however, so I finally gave in. It was there that I first fully desired a new life. Love and enthusiasm for Christ vibrated off all the "religious people." Instead of an atmosphere of "who's cool and who's not" which had been my previous perspective, the attitude was "everyone is cool" because we are brothers and sisters in Christ

Jesus. I saw my "fun" life for what it really was—shallow and empty. How could it be otherwise without God?

I took theology classes at St. Lawrence Center and spent more and more time in prayer. At first, I still struggled with a faith in Jesus as truly the Son of God. Finally, I received the last push I needed to accept Jesus as God. I was shown that Jesus really did claim to be the Son of God, so either He was God's Son or He was a liar or a lunatic.

Even the best scam artist could not convince crowds that they had filled up on loaves and fishes that were multiplied. Nor could someone trick the dead into rising or lepers to heal withered limbs. Either these things happened or they did not. I came to understand that there is more historical evidence to support the writings of the New Testament than many "historical" events that we accept as fact.

My doubts and emptiness faded as I became filled with a rich faith in Jesus. Not only did I attend Mass on Sundays, but I began to go daily, to pray and worship my Lord, who had lifted me out of darkness.

It was during my religious journey that the focus on my art began to change. First, I copied Rubens' painting *Samson and Delilah* for class. The fabrics and textures fascinated me. Next, I did *The Raising of the Cross,* also by Rubens. Students and instructors expressed awe at my ability to copy the emotion and movement.

On my own, I did a sketch of St. Maximilian Kolbe, a man who loved enough to give his life in exchange for another at a German concentration camp during World War II. I went on to sketch other religious heroes. My religious devotion and artistic talents were becoming one. Painting and sketching subjects that reflected God's love became my focus.

Although some instructors were encouraging, not all were impressed. One instructor went so far as to refuse to work with me. But it did not matter to me. I was near graduation, and by then knew that my life would be dedicated to serving God. I had come to realize that although beauty created by my hands cannot compare to the beauty of God, I desired that my art would help lead others to a deeper love for our Lord.

Though God was in my life, I still had the urgent question after graduation of "what now?" I was working at a Hobby Lobby store to pay my bills, but I was still unsure of where my life would take me. I was getting irritated because, after putting in a hard day's work, there seemed to be little time for my painting.

But God always has a plan and will always let you know what it is if you trust in Him. I now know that before He could show me my path, He needed me to accept something. Though I kept painting religious scenes, I began to doubt that I would ever be able to make a living at it. I prayed for God's guidance, and I came to realize that it did not matter if I made a lot of money at it or no money at all. I knew that regardless of commercial success, it was all about painting for God.

After I accepted whatever outcome my painting would bring, I sold my reproduction of Rubens' *Rising of the Cross* for $5,000! Shortly after this success, I was approached by John from an apostolate called School of Faith, which provides religious educational classes. He wanted to commission me to do artwork for a Catholic academy. He asked me how long it would take for me to do scenes from the Joyful and Glorious Mysteries of the Rosary. I told him that because of my job at the hobby store, it would probably take at least two years.

"Well," he told me, "it sounds like the hobby store is getting in your way. Why don't you get rid of it and work for me full time? I could probably set you up with a studio in the high school."

I was amazed. I had put my talent in God's hands, and He did the rest. This was in 2005. I am still working for John today, who has provided me an outlet for my religious artwork.

So now, I paint in a style that reflects my faith journey. Although Jesus and His holy ones are far above our earthly world, they were also once in it. I paint them as I imagine they might have been when they walked the earth. Even God, who is our Creator, became one of us. He loved us enough to send His only begotten Son to be born of a woman and walk the earth with His beloved creatures. This is what I try to capture in my pictures, the closeness and realness of God and His loved ones.

— Jason Jenicke

Since 2001, Jason Jenicke's mission has been to continue using his talents to create art that helps draw others to a more personal relationship with God. Before each piece of art he creates, Jason studies what he is depicting to help capture the emotion, culture, and feel of the event. He then prays and has faith that our Lord will continue to guide him to help glorify God and His Son. To view Jason's work, go to www.jasonjenicke.com.

Providential Cookies and Rent

In the fall of 2007, a prayer and fasting vigil called Forty Days for Life was held in eighty-nine cities and thirty-one states across the country. People prayed and fasted for forty days for an end to abortion in our nation. Approximately 350 babies were documented as being saved.

When it was announced that Forty Days for Life was going to be held again in the spring of 2008, I instantly wanted to sign up. We had a few things to think about, though. My husband had been a real estate agent and had not had any business for months. He was finally blessed with a job working at a restaurant, but the pay was only about one-sixth of what he had been making. To sign up to coordinate a Forty Days for Life vigil meant spending $197 for the packet. That was about all the money we had in the bank, and it had already been spoken for by all our bills.

The final day to sign up arrived. I knew I wanted to do this, but we did not have enough money to pay for the Forty Days for Life packet and pay the bills. I asked my husband what he thought and he said, "If you believe God is calling you to do this, then sign up, and God will provide the money to pay the bills."

I was so excited. I ran to the computer, signed up, typed in my debit card number, and watched as all but a few dollars that we had disappear from our bank account. It was the greatest feeling in the world—and, at the same time, I began to wonder what I had just done.

The next day I was scheduled to sell cookies for a fundraiser for a friend. I told God that if I sold every cookie that I had baked, I would make $206, which would cover the cost of the Forty Days for Life materials.

The afternoon was a nightmare. I had fallen asleep while baking the cookies and burned two dozen. I wanted to get to the school early but arrived late. Anything that could go wrong did. I just kept repeating to myself, "God can do anything. Never give up."

I set up the table and tried to keep the wind from blowing everything away. Then people started buying dozens of cookies. I would try to give them their change only to be told to keep it. One lady came with an envelope full of money. Another woman came to me with a check and said, "Which ones do you recommend?" I looked at the check and saw that it was for $500! I told her she could take all of them. She took two dozen, gave me a hug, and was on her way. By the end of the afternoon I still had dozens of cookies—and $903!

I have been baking cookies as gifts for my husband's real estate clients for years. People often suggested that I sell them. We tried to get a license to do so, but there was so much red tape and many expenses, so we couldn't do it. I learned that I could, however, sell them as a fundraiser item. My friend had asked me to bake the cookies for teachers' gifts and also for her son's eighth grade fundraiser for a trip to Washington, D.C. She told me that if I made the cookies for the gifts and gave her five percent of the proceeds from the cookies for her son and five percent to the school, I could keep the rest for myself.

At the end of the day, I gave $100 to the principal for the school and the D.C. trip, and the rest I took home and used it to pay a myriad of bills. The school ended up giving me the $100 back as well. They knew our financial situation and wanted us to have the money. As I look back, I believe my friend's intention was to advertise my cookies so that others would order more, and we would have a little additional income. That is exactly what happened. I received many orders for Christmas gifts.

I believe God was confirming what I already believed He was asking us to do. I went home and told my husband what had happened. He too, was stunned. We said a prayer of thanksgiving and began to plan for the Forty Days for Life campaign.

I sent out an e-mail telling everyone I could think of about Forty Days for Life and invited them to an informational meeting at my house. Sixteen people from around the Phoenix area attended. The first of the Forty Days for Life was just twenty-two days away, and we had lots of work to do. The next few weeks are but a flurry of memories: notes, phone calls, e-mails, and many, many sleepless nights.

We did finally make it to that first day of the prayer vigil. It was so exciting. A friend who was leading the vigil near my home prayed with me from midnight to 1:00 a.m. on the very first day. We also signed up to pray during the final hour of the last day. It was a symbol of the fact that we were in this for the long haul.

After a few days, though, reality began to set in. I had not told anyone that we were unable to make our house payments. We had not made a payment in more than seven months. We had tried to work with the mortgage company to lower our payment, but the company would not budge. In late January, we received a letter stating that our home would go up for public auction on February 11, 2008, just five days after the forty days were set to begin. On that day, our home was sold back to the bank. We thought that we might be able to stay for a while since the housing market was so slow, but that was not the case. Five days later, we received an eviction notice to get out in five days or we would be charged rent at the highest possible rate.

During all of this, I decided I needed to inform the national leader of Forty Days for Life, David Bereit, of our situation and hand the coordinator position over to Arizona Right to Life. I would soon not have a computer, and did not know if I would even have a home. Right to Life agreed to take the helm.

We continued to go to Planned Parenthood every day to pray for an end to abortion. On one beautiful evening when our family was out praying, a couple pulled up to Planned Parenthood. They drove up to the door, got out of their car, looked at each other, and looked at my son, who was holding a sign with an 800-number and a message of hope. They got back in their car, drove up to my son, gave him the thumbs up sign, took down the number, and drove away. That alone was worth every dime we had spent.

Yet, we would soon have no home. Many of our friends had offered to let us stay with them, but we declined, concerned that this would be too much strain on a friendship. We were prepared to stay in our van for a few nights, but that did not become necessary. A fellow homeschooler was told of our situation, and just happened to have a vacant house located not far from where we lived. They offered to let us stay there until we found something more permanent. We were so very grateful for their offer and God's provision.

As we were packing up, I had a moment of feeling totally overwhelmed by our whole situation. We had to pack our entire home and eight kids and move into a house a few miles down the road, only to do it all over again in the near future. I submitted it all to God and said, "Thy will be done. Do with us as you will."

Just then the phone rang. I answered, "Hello, how may I help you?" It was our pastor.

He replied, "The question is, 'How may I help you?'" He was calling to tell us that someone from the church had heard of our situation and had offered to pay our rent. The family who owned the home was starting to feel the financial crunch of having two properties. They had moved to be closer to their children's school, and the home they were offering to us had not yet sold. God in His mercy provided for both of us: He gave us a place to stay, and He gave the owners a house payment that they needed. Who could have imagined?

As I continue to pray for an end to abortion, I never forget that God is always faithful; He will always take care of us in a way that He knows is best for us.

— Anita Usher

Anita Usher is a homeschooling mother of eight who has a passion for writing and speaking for the unborn and their families. For more information, you can go to www.40daysforlife.com to find out how you can be involved in praying and fasting for an end to abortion.

Everyday Hero

It is not always an easy commitment to keep, but I try never to get mad at anyone, not even for a short time. Life is short. This was one of the things I came to understand on October 20, 2003, when my life took a dramatic change. On that day, I came to understand the value of human life and the ability of ordinary people to do extraordinary things when the situation calls for it.

My wife and I live in Grass Lake, Michigan. We both work in Lansing, where our two boys go to school. On an average day, my wife takes the boys to school, and I drive separately a little later to my accounting job. That was our routine that day in October. Fall was in full swing, with most of the trees having dropped half their leaves.

I progressed slowly along the stalled traffic in my Volkswagen Beetle when, in an instant, came a sound that would forever separate this day from all others. I heard a loud crash behind me and looked quickly in my rearview mirror. To my horror I saw a semi-truck with flames shooting about fifty feet into the air headed directly towards me. This got the backed-up traffic moving, and I hurried to get myself out of the way. As my foot reached for the gas, my car stalled! I restarted my car to get out of the way. The semi came to a violent stop twenty to thirty feet behind my vehicle.

Immediately, I took out my cell phone and called 911. The response from the operator indicated that others had already called. The traffic ahead of me was no longer stalled, leaving me a clear path to continue on to work. I hesitated for a moment. *Do I keep driving to work or get out to see if there is anything I can do to help?* I questioned. The inner voice of self-doubt told me that I was not a doctor, so there would be no reason for me to get out of my car. *No*, I argued with myself, *I need to see if there's something I can do to help.*

I pulled my car off to the side of the road and put on the

emergency brake. I quickly hopped the median strip to approach the crash. It seemed that there were people running around everywhere as the flames shot up from the crash of the semi. Getting closer, I saw that there was more than just the semi involved in the accident. The big truck had smashed into the back of a suburban. From twenty feet away from the wreckage, I felt an intense heat radiating as flames shot out of the window of the suburban.

"Help me!" came a desperate scream from the vehicle. I realized in horror that there was a man trapped inside the suburban with the upper half of his body hanging out of the shattered window. His eyes were looking right at me as he screamed: "Help me!" Flames were shooting out from behind this poor man. Two men had just given up trying to pull him out of the car, and everyone in the area looked on in despair. Some people were trying to put the flames out with fire extinguishers, but I could see from the intensity of the fire that such action would be as futile as trying to chop down an oak with a butter knife.

My mind raced as time stopped and seconds passed like eons. The door seemed slightly ajar, and I thought we might be able to rip it off. "Someone get me a chain!" I yelled decisively. A few seconds passed like hours as a man seemed to approach me in slow motion holding a chain he had retrieved from a trailer. Some people were still running around spraying fire extinguishers.

People watched helplessly as I tried to loop the door with the chain. I threw the chain and missed. I felt frantic, sensing the urgent weight of each passing second. There was no time for error. A man's life literally burning up. He was going to die unless someone could do something quickly. My second attempt succeeded in getting the chain around the car door. The man was losing consciousness. I could not get close to the vehicle without becoming a victim of the flames myself. With the chain looped around the door, I took both ends and began to pull with everything I had. At that moment, two men appeared beside me to help. The inside of the vehicle was a white melt of heat. People who had previously been standing helpless now saw that action could be taken. Two men ran up again to try to drag the man out of his car. This time, they succeeded and dragged him out onto the interstate.

Most of his clothes had been burned off, and the remaining rags of a shirt were still aflame. What was left, fire extinguishers were used to quench the flames on the man. Things inside the vehicle kept exploding, and out of fear that a blast could reach us, the man was dragged further away from the car. One kind man bent down to the head of the burned victim and started consoling him.

I remembered from my CPR class that water was most effective in treating burns, so I yelled, "Does anybody have water?" A woman emerged with a wicker basket filled with water bottles. The story of the loaves and the fishes flashed in my mind as I opened one of the bottles.

As I went to administer the water, an ambulance arrived, but it stopped some two hundred feet from where the man lay. I sprinted down the road and motioned and yelled for the ambulance to come this way. By this time, the fire department had arrived and were putting out the fire. The two vehicles that moments before had been engulfed in an inferno were now a mass of steam.

I found myself in a group of several men—other men who had helped with the chain and dragged the man out of the car. We formed a silent circle; any possible words were swallowed up by raw emotions. A man walked up to us, and in a cynical tone said, "We gotta get these big cars off the road. See what they cause?"

When I heard such insensitive and harsh words, I thought, *How could he not see how inappropriate they were?* Then, as if to counteract them, one of the men patted me on the back and said, "That was a really great idea with the chain."

As time seemed to resume its normal pace and the surge of adrenaline abated, my forehead started burning. I went over to one of the many paramedics, and he looked at it and said, "Looks like you caught a little bit of a burn there."

He gave me a water-soaked towel to put on it just as a helicopter arrived to take the injured man to the University of Michigan burn center. Though my forehead continued to burn and I was mentally shaken, I felt fine overall. But when one of the paramedics asked me if I wanted to go to the hospital in Jackson, I thought it would probably be a good idea.

In the ambulance, I called my work to say that I would be late. It turned out that I had second-degree burns on my forehead and all of my skin had bubbled up into one big mass of blisters— the body's natural way of dealing with burns.

As I was being bandaged up, a doctor came in and shook my hand. "I wanted to shake the hand of a hero," he said. I looked at him, shocked; I did not think of myself a hero. The hospital in Jackson made an appointment for me at the University of Michigan burn center because the doctors thought I should go in to have my burns looked at.

Since I had left my car at the side of the interstate, my wife drove me to my parents' house so that they could take me to my car. I told them the story of what had happened.

"Why did you do this?" they asked. "Didn't you know that you could have been hurt?"

I considered this, but realized I was not thinking about my own safety at the time. All I was thinking was that if that had been me in the car I would have wanted someone to be there to try his or her best to help me.

At the accident scene, a policeman had been posted to keep people away. My dad and I drove up with my head all bandaged up and I explained to him that I had been there earlier in the day and that I had come to get my car. "Yes, I know," he said. "Do you know you are a hero?"

This was the second time I had been called a hero that day, and it made me uncomfortable. After the accident, I was interviewed by the local news, and later that year, along with some of the other men who helped, I received the American Red Cross' award for Everyday Heroes. It was at the awards ceremony that I met the wife and kids of the man I had helped. Eighty percent of his body had been burned, and he passed away eight months after the accident. I was glad that through my efforts and the efforts of others, he had died peacefully in bed rather than in that terrible inferno. I was most touched by his mother, who called me her angel.

As a lifelong Catholic, I have always had an appreciation and reverence for life in all its stages. It is humbling to realize that if I had left for work that October morning mere moments later, it likely could have been me trapped inside those vicious flames. The frailty of life is sometimes a hard fact to accept, but mostly it makes us appreciate every moment that we have without family and friends, knowing that at any moment God may call us home.

I have also come to realize that a hero is not always some superhero figure who rescues people from danger on a daily basis. No, a hero is someone who loves life, and when the opportunity to help someone continue living is presented, will do everything in his power to preserve life.

— Chet Czubko, Jr.

Chet Czubko, Jr., is a graduate of Michigan State University and works as a certified public accountant. He has served as a church organist for more than forty years and is currently the organist and choir director at Our Lady of Fatima Parish in Michigan Center, Michigan. Chet and his father have been inducted into the Michigan Polka Music Hall of Fame.

Chapter 2

With God All Things Are Possible

The Road to the Rebels

I grew up in a country I loved, surrounded by a family I cherished. But in 1994, my idyllic world was ripped apart as Rwanda descended into a bloody genocide. My family was brutally murdered during a killing spree that lasted three months and claimed the lives of nearly a million Rwandans.

Miraculously, I survived the slaughter. For ninety-one days, seven other women and I huddled silently together in the cramped bathroom of a local pastor's home while hundreds of machete-wielding killers hunted for us.

It was during those endless hours of unspeakable terror that I learned the power of prayer, eventually shedding my fear of death and forging a profound and lasting relationship with God. I talked with God and prayed endlessly. There were times when I heard the voice of the devil, taunting and mocking my faith. After all, my situation seemed hopeless, and so many around me were being killed. *Where was God in all of this?* But I also heard the voice of God and persevered in prayer, holding onto my faith. But there was one spiritual hurdle that seemed insurmountable— to forgive the members of the Hutus tribe responsible for the horrific genocide. *How could I forgive and love the bloodthirsty killers who had destroyed my beloved family and way of life? How could I give love in the face of such intense hatred?*

It seemed I did not have such love within me, yet I understood that God's command was that we love one another. Through almost constant prayer, I progressed in my faith and came to see that the killers were like foolish children. The Hutus had convinced themselves that the Tutsis were lower than animals, bent on overpowering and destroying the other tribe. With this misperception, the Hutus set off a spree of murder in which the crime of being born a Tutsi was punishable by immediate death.

When I finally emerged from the bathroom hideout, I had truly discovered the meaning of an unconditional love so strong that I was able to forgive my family's killers. But thrown into sudden freedom under the cover of darkness, with no protection and surrounded by killers, I had to struggle against seemingly impossible odds to save my life.

Stretching for the first time in months and feeling the cool night air against my skin, I filled my lungs with fresh air and gazed upon the brilliant, hypnotic beauty of the countless stars above. My soul sang out, "Praise God!"

The other women escaping from the bathroom with me made it to a camp that French soldiers had set up to offer outside protection in the midst of this civil war. I understood French and became a translator for the group. Our rescuers explained that we were in a field encampment and that a truck would transfer us to the base camp ten miles away.

At the base camp I learned the painful truth about my family—they had all been killed. While I had been hiding in the bathroom, Jesus had told me in prayer that they would all be dead, but there was a part of me that had hoped it would not be so. I cried until there were no tears left. Then I prayed: "They are all dead. Everything I loved in this world has been taken away. I'm putting my life in your hands, Jesus. Keep your promise and take care of me. I will keep my promise. I will be your faithful daughter." Then I closed my eyes and pictured my family and realized how alone in the world I was now.

I was soon transferred with a truckload of others to another

French camp, which was a fort that kept the Hutus out and the Tutsis in. Although the soldiers often apologized for the deplorable condition, to me, breathing fresh air and falling asleep on the ground under the stars was like seeing the face of God. On a diet of cheese and crackers, powdered milk, and canned fruit, I began adding pounds onto my skeleton-like frame. The soldiers said it was their job to protect the Tutsis. Sometimes, gangs of Hutus would gather outside the camp perimeter and stare at as if they were looking at zoo animals—amazed that there were still Tutsis alive.

The captain of the camp was especially sympathetic. "They're monsters!" he said of the Hutus. Then he offered me something that was hard to resist: "If you want revenge, it's yours for the asking," he said. "Give me the names of the Hutus who were searching for you, or the ones who killed your parents and brothers, and I'll have them killed for you."

It was exactly what I had wished for during the early days in the cramped bathroom, when the pastor who hid me had told me of the atrocities. I had wanted vengeance so badly, but God had opened my heart, and I had made peace with my killers. I slipped my hand into my pocket and fingered my father's rosary, the one item I had been able to keep with me through it all.

"Well, Hutus aren't evil, Captain. It's just these killers. They've been tricked by the devil ... they've wandered away from God," I tried to tell him.

The captain was incredulous, insisting that the Hutus were evil and deserved death. I again declined and prayed that God would touch the Captain's heart with his forgiveness. I prayed again that the Hutus would put down their machetes and beg for God's mercy.

Listening to the heartbreaking stories of others, I often forgot my own pain. It was the children who tried to comfort each other that broke my heart the most. Watching one little boy cradle his younger brother and promise that everything would be better

when Mommy and Daddy came to get them, I knew that one
of the reasons I had been spared was to later help the children
orphaned by the genocide and steer them away from the hatred
that had robbed them of a family's love.

But just as I began to feel hopeful that the worst of the danger
was behind me, the French pulled out and abandoned us. On
a hot afternoon in late August, the French captain notified me
that we were being evicted that very day and the French were
preparing to leave Rwanda. The soldiers said they would take
the thirty refugees to a Tutsi military camp a few miles down
the road so that we could be with our own people. I was relieved
to learn that the Tutsis were fighting their way back into the
country. I had even heard that soon the genocide would be over.

Climbing into the back of a truck, I fingered my rosary and
said a prayer that God would shepherd us safely to the Tutsi
camp. A canvas tarp was rolled over the back to conceal the
precious cargo. The truck pulled past the semicircle of armored
vehicles, down a service road, and into a sea of killers. Through
a crack in the tarp, I saw thousands of Hutus carrying machetes
and trudging along the main road toward Lake Kivu.

"Oh, God," I said, falling back in the truck. "Not again!
Please, God," I prayed. "You have brought us this far—now take
us the rest of the way. Blind these killers ... don't let them look in
the back of this truck. Merciful God, shield us from their hateful
eyes!" More than halfway to the RPF camp the truck stopped,
and the French captain pulled the tarp open. "We have reports
of gunfire in the area, and we have orders to avoid fighting at
any cost. We're turning around. This is where you'll have to get
out."

"Please, Captain, you know better than anyone what will
happen if you leave us here. There are killers all around us!
Please, I'm begging you. Take us another mile to the RPF camp
or take us back with you. Don't leave us here to be killed!"

No amount of begging could get him to change his mind.

"Get out of the truck," I said to my friends. "Everybody out. The French are leaving us here."

The cries of disbelief and fear coming from the back of the truck drew even more attention from the killers, who were now moving toward us. I looked one Interahamwe straight in the eye and held his gaze. My heart told me that he was a person just like me, and that he really didn't want to kill. I held my rosary and summoned all my will to send a message of love to him. I prayed that God would use me to touch the killer with the power of His love.

I didn't blink ... and we stared into each other's eyes for what seemed like a lifetime. Finally, the killer broke my gaze and looked away. He turned his back to me and dropped his machete, as if the devil had left his body. But there were plenty of other devils to take his place. At least fifteen Interahamwe were now standing a few yards from the truck with machetes in their hands and hatred on their faces. They were figuring out what was happening, waiting to see if any of my companions would dare leave the truck.

We had no choice but to come out. One by one, my friends jumped out, until all thirty of us were standing there facing the killers. Two French soldiers lifted down my friend Aloise, who was a mother of two in a wheelchair. They then pulled away at high speed.

"Look at all these Tutsis," one of the killers said in amazement. "How can it be that they're still alive?"

"These are the cockroaches that the French soldiers were protecting," another said. "Who's going to save you now, cockroaches?"

"Let's go," I said. "We'll walk to the RPF camp—their soldiers are close by." The killers heard me mention the RPF and got nervous. We began moving but didn't get too far. The road was so strewn with rocks and bodies that it was practically impossible to push Aloise's wheelchair. When a wheel became stuck in a rut, we all stopped. Aloise's children were also crying and clutching their mother's arms.

I pulled my friends Jean Paul and Karega away from the group. "You two come with me. The rest of you stay with Aloise ... and pray. I'll find the Tutsi soldiers and come back with help. Don't move from this spot, or I won't be able to find you in the middle of all these Hutu refugees."

With that, I struck out in the direction that the French had been taking us before they abandoned us. As we walked, I prayed my rosary, talking to God with all my heart and soul: "God, I really am walking through the valley of death—please stay with me. Shield me with the power of your love. You created this ground that we're walking on, so please don't let these killers spill your daughter's blood on it." Three Interahamwe followed us as we broke away from the larger group, and one of them recognized me. "I know this cockroach," he said. "This is Leonard's daughter. We've been looking for her for months! I can't believe she's still alive. We killed the rest of them, but this little cockroach gave us the slip!"

"Dear God," I prayed, walking as fast as I could and holding my father's rosary rightly in my hand. "Only You can save me. You promised to take care of me, God—well, I really need taking care of right now. There are devils and vultures at my back, Lord. Please protect me. Take the evil from the hearts of these men, and blind their hatred with Your holy love."

I walked without looking at my feet, not knowing if I was about to stumble over rocks or bodies, putting all my trust in God to guide me to safety. We were moving very briskly, but the killers were all around us now, circling us, slicing the air with their machetes. We were defenseless, so why were they waiting to strike?

"If they kill me, God, I ask You to forgive them. Their hearts have been corrupted by hatred, and they don't know why they want to hurt me."

After walking a half mile like that, I heard Jean Paul say, "Hey, they're gone ... they're gone!"

I looked around, and it was true. The killers had left us. Jean Paul said later that it was probably because they knew the RPF soldiers were close by, but I knew the real reason, and I never stopped thanking God for saving us on that road. A few minutes later we saw an RPF roadblock and several dozen tall, lean, stone-faced Tutsi soldiers standing guard. I broke into an all-out run and dropped to my knees in front of them. I closed my eyes and sang their praises.

"Thank God, thank God, we're saved! Thank God you're here. Bless you! Bless you all!

— Immaculée Ilibagiza

Immaculée Ilibagiza was born in Rwanda and studied electronic and mechanical engineering at the National University. She lost most of her family during the 1994 genocide. Four years later, she emigrated to the United States and began working for the United Nations in New York City. She has since authored the New York Times *best-selling book* Left to Tell: Discovering God Amidst the Rwandan Holocaust, *which has sold more than 250,000 copies, been made into a documentary, and raised money for orphans of Rwanda. She has established the Left to Tell Charitable Fund to help others heal from the long-term effects of genocide and war. Ms. Ilibagiza has been invited to speak to a range of audiences, including dignitaries of the world, multinational corporations, churches, and local school children. Immaculée now lives in Manhattan with her husband and their two children. For more information, visit www.lefttotell.com.*

Lion! Oh My!

After two years without a vacation, my trip to Montana's Glacier National Park in the Rocky Mountains was supplying me with a much-needed break from a busy life in the Chicago area. Not even the small setbacks of losing luggage or having a horse back riding reservation canceled were able to dampen the enjoyment of being so present in such a gorgeous place.

Instead of taking the horseback-riding tour I had planned on, I opted to do a solo hike up the six-and-a-half mile Sperry Trail. While I had read it was inadvisable to go alone, I was comforted when the stable manager assured me that a bear had not been sighted since March in the area. He told me the most I might see at this time of year would be some mountain goats.

I started the hike energized and enthusiastic. This was going to be a great day in a great place. The bear bells I contemplated not taking were tucked in my jean pockets so that their noise would not take away from the sounds of nature. After only forty-five minutes, I heard the distant jingle of bells heralding two college students who overtook me, greeting me warmly as I passed. It was a comfort not being completely alone on the trail in case a bear was in the neighborhood.

For the next several hours there was a reasonable amount of activity on the trail as hikers, trekking at a pace much faster than I was, passed me as they rushed to distant destinations in hopes of arriving before dark. I, on the other hand, took my time so as to relish each moment. The smell of pines mixed with the distant splash of glacier-fed waterfalls gave me a radiant sense of peace and serenity that nourished my spirit.

Toward midday, I sat to rest on a large rock jutting out into the trail. Instead of taking my camcorder out of my backpack, I looked up the trail and made a mental picture of everything. I could see where the thick ground cover tapered off where the tree line ended. With several deep breaths and one refreshing drink of water, I decided it was time to start my hike back.

In the first few steps of my return, something made me stop. The quiet, pensive demeanor I had been carefully cultivating for the past four hours gave way to surging adrenaline and an audible heartbeat. There in the trail, ten meters in front of me, was a mountain lion. My mind desperately searched for memories of what to do in this situation. Should I run? Walk? Play dead? Make noise? Walk toward it? Run away from it? Throw something at it? Its eyes seemed to be cunningly evaluating me from the short distance in front of me.

All I could think of was how to handle an encounter with a bear. I remembered the advice to "get large, make noise, and throw things." I picked up a large rock and threw it towards the cat. It thumped pitifully short of the target. So I put on my bear bells as I continued shouting at the cat. Then, the cat disappeared, leaving a frightened silence.

Knowing it was unwise to stay, I picked up two rocks, and began a hurried descent down the trail. After going forty feet down the trail, I turned to assess my surroundings and make sure that the cat had not returned. In that instant I screamed and ran backwards several steps, yelling for help. The lion was just off the trail a foot from where I had stood. It was crouched low in the brush. As it came onto the trail, I continued to yell and threw a rock that just barely missed the animal. The cat again disappeared, leaving me much more frightened than the first time. This mountain lion was stalking me. I could see it thirty feet up the trail, crouching behind a rock. Was it waiting for me? I did not want to find out. A second later it was no longer behind the rock. I saw a glimpse of it much closer up the trail. For several minutes the cat would disappear entirely, and then I would catch momentary glimpses of it approaching me from off the trail. I was alone and scared. What could I do? Where could I go? Fear and exhaustion drained me physically. I could not outrun this animal and could certainly not overpower it. I continued to yell for help that I suspected would not come.

Heartrending thoughts began bouncing through my head as my mind rushed to conclusions. I thought of the family I would not be able to say good-bye to, the granddaughter I would not watch grow up. Was I to become nothing more than a rare statistic of fatal mountain lion attacks? Suddenly, it dawned on me that there was one thing I had not done yet: pray.

I began to pray out loud, and as I did, my fear lifted. Suddenly, my situation did not feel so dire. Nothing had changed but my assessment of it. I could die. I knew that so clearly. But a calm reassurance that I was not alone comforted me. There was more than just me and a lion here. I suddenly saw that the control we think we have is mostly an illusion. My fate was in God's hands, and I was ready to accept His will, whatever it was.

As I prayed aloud, the lion reemerged from his hiding place a mere three feet in front of me. I looked at this beautiful, terrible beast as it stood staring back at me. My sweaty palm gripped a rock, and I steadied myself for a final throw. Something told me that if I missed now, it would be all over. I released the rock, and it hit the cat squarely on its shoulder. The cat jumped back and retreated into the forest. A second rock hit it in the hind quarter as it made its retreat.

For the rest of the three-hour hike back, I prayed that the cat would not return. It did not. Exhausted and thankful to be back, I reported the incident to the ranger station and gladly went back to the security of my room.

After the incident, I contemplated whether it was faith that had saved me or God's love that had allowed me to have such a dramatic experience with one of His magnificent creatures. The experience was short, probably a mere twelve minutes. But time is not the yardstick for measuring such experiences. While I truly considered that I might not make it off that mountain, it was my prayers that gave me the peace to accept either outcome.

– Peggy M. Podboy

Peggy Podboy was diagnosed with breast cancer in 1991. Over the next eight years, she underwent mastectomies, multiple rounds of chemotherapy, radiation, and two bone marrow transplants. A single mother to her only child, Jim, she became a grandmother in 1995, just six weeks before her fateful encounter with the mountain lion in Montana. Peggy lived a full life in her short fifty years and passed away in 1999, surrounded by those she loved. Her strength and resolve both on the mountain and in the life she led set examples for all of those who knew her.

Safe Harbor

Chuong Nguyen felt a sour stinging in his stomach as he watched the Malaysian authorities fire torpedoes at the forty-foot fishing boat that moments earlier had carried his hopes and dreams for the future. The initial blasts shone powerfully and then dissipated as the sinking vessel disappeared, leaving foamy waves—the last remnants of sunken dreams.

This was his fourth attempt of escape from South Vietnam, and, as with the previous three, all Chuong's carefully laid plans were beginning to unravel. On previous failed attempts, his options had not left him with such a "what now?" angst. In one attempt, he had been placed in a metal cargo box for three days underneath a relentless tropical sun. While in the box his choices had been black and white: give into torturing and reveal the identity of who had organized the escape, or remain silent and wait for rescue. Rescue from the metal box came in the form of a bribe from his family.

On this most recent attempt, Chuong's options seemed limited to either a successful attempt or death. He was soon to turn eighteen, and Communist Army draftees faced unnerving odds of survival on the dire Laotian war front.

With such uninspiring prospects looming in his near future, he and his brother had fled in the mask of night with nothing more than a change of clothes and a gold ring given to them by their mother to use when needed.

Making it aboard the now sunken fishing boat had been no easy task. At stake for getting caught was death or torture in a jail. The Vietnam they were living in was not the idyllic one in the memories of their youth. After Saigon fell, the totalitarian Communist regime that took power forbade religious freedom and demanded obedience only to Ho Chi Minh.

Chuong had spent the past seven days aboard the fishing vessel along with forty-five other refugees packed like sardines in a tiny compartment under its cabin. Though such quarters reminded him of his time locked in the small metal box, these close quarters had a purpose beyond causing suffering. The potential of a better life was linked to the affliction.

Thankfully, he and his brother had reached Malaysia before their boat's destruction. Though previously disposed to accepting Vietnamese refugees, Malaysia had begun to quarantine them to protect its own population from both overpopulating areas and from diseases that refugees often carried with them.

Chuong and his brother were taken to a refugee camp overpopulated with refugees and understaffed by U.N. workers. Beyond the water and food supplied once a week, little else was provided at the camp. Chuong started his life outside Vietnam owning only the pair of shorts he wore.

His life in the camp was far from easy, as judged by Western standards. For six months he slept on the roof of a shack underneath a tarp. However, the lack of comforts was of little consequence, as such things were not of importance for the journey he wished to embark upon. What Chuong lacked in materials he made up for in desire. He and his brother had applied for asylum in the United States and spent their days patiently waiting for a response. Because they had such hope in the future, each day was one day closer to redemption. Not being able to make things happen on his own in the camp, Chuong spent much of his time imploring God's intervention. At times he felt alone, as though his words never made it beyond the camp.

After eight months of waiting, deliverance came for Chuong and his brother. They finally received word that they were accepted! They moved to California in 1982, where several of their cousins, also refugees, lived.

In the refugee camp, Chuong had only been able to hope and pray for redemption. Now that his liberation had come, success rested upon his shoulders. In California, he worked tirelessly as a waiter to send money back to his parents so that they, too, could escape as refugees. Within the year, his parents were able to escape. A church in Michigan agreed to sponsor them, so Chuong relocated to Michigan, where he enrolled in college.

At times, while he was in school, everything seemed impossible. He often struggled to understand the subjects due to his limited English. Chuong was working full time and still not able to make ends meet. It was during such times that everything seemed overwhelming. That is when he began to spend time in adoration before the Blessed Sacrament. Sitting in front of Jesus in the Eucharist was not time spent away from his other necessary tasks, but rather the time when he was given the strength to deal with them. He would arrive at adoration exhausted and tell God simply that he had given up; it was just too much. As time passed in the presence of Jesus, his frantic thoughts would return to his desperate days in the refugee camp, when he slept underneath a tarp on top of a hut. Then he would remember what the fishing boat looked like when it was torpedoed. He would remember what it felt like to be trapped in a metal box underneath a spitefully hot sun.

Eventually, Chuong would look up at the host and say to Jesus, "I have already come this far. I don't think I can go farther. God, if you want me to go on, please help me because I don't feel I have the strength to do it."

In the end, Chuong not only had the strength to go through with everything, but his faith gave him the fortitude to excel. His hard work allowed him not only to assist financially in his mother's redemption, but also to also receive a degree in computer information systems and a grade point average of 3.46. Chuong has gone from being locked in a metal box in Vietnam's hundred degree heat, uncertain of life or death, to becoming an American citizen in 1992. He is now married and the father two beautiful daughters.

When questioned about his success, Chuong is quick to thank God and point to the many who were not as fortunate to escape. He then humbly explains that, even though at times he wondered where God was in his life, he now sees that God was always there helping him to succeed against all odds. Now he feels God is calling him to become a shining light to others facing dire situations.

— Luke Armstrong

Chuong Nguyen lives with his wife and two daughters in Mason, Michigan. He works for the Ingham Regional Medical Center as a supervisor in the engineering department.

Luke Armstrong is a co-editor of Amazing Grace for Survivors. *His biography appears at the end of the book.*

All the World's a Stage

A mother watched helplessly as her five-year-old child tossed feebly in his bed. The fever had just reached 105 degrees, and the darkest fear of a mother filled her. He could die from the fever, and there seemed little that anyone could do. "Oh, please God, please help my son," she prayed, choking back the tears. "Oh, Mary, mother of God, pray for us, please."

The forlorn mother picked up a prayer book and began a holy hour of prayers for a dying child. She looked down at the prayer to consecrate the life of a child to the Blessed Mother and slowly raised her hands above her suffering child as she recited it. She paused in mid-sentence before continuing the final verse, "I relinquish every single right as a mother, naturally and spiritually. And if you so choose to take his life and end it now, I completely give you my son."

Many years later...

The back of my mind seemed a good place to put God for the time being. I was acting in and directing shows and performing in front of adoring crowds from Los Angeles to San Francisco. Along with all the singing, performing, and acting came a whole lot of money. It would have been hard to afford such a sinful life as I was leading without all that money. Though I was raised a Catholic in Milwaukee, there was little evidence of this in my life.

Drifting from the Church had not been a conscious decision; it just happened. My favorite Christmas present when I was a young boy was a priest suit. There was never any doubt in my mind that I would serve God as one of his priests. But then, a crushing blow ended that dream. When I applied to attend St. Francis DeSales High School Seminary in the eighth grade, I was told that my parents' divorce was an impediment to the priesthood. Not even on the day they married did my father have any intention of being faithful to my mother. Many years later, she was granted an annulment, but at the time, being from a broken family closed the door on my dream to become a priest. (This impediment would later be lifted following the Second Vatican Council.) Instead, I determined that the stage would be my pulpit. It would be a way to reach people. Despite being a shy introvert, I pushed myself to get up on stage at every opportunity. Unfortunately, along the way, I had forgotten the part about serving God.

One particular day, while walking through Los Angeles on the way to a rehearsal, I passed a church. I must have walked by it a hundred times without ever noticing it, but it suddenly stood out at me. Looking up to the bell tower, an intense desire beckoned me inside. I decided to step inside for a bit before my rehearsal. Opening the door to the dimly lit building, I could not remember the last time I had been inside a church. A statue of Mary decked out with flowers and incense immediately caught my attention. I mechanically knelt down and prayed.

As I prayed, a subtle desire nudged at me. I could not identify it at first, but as it grew, I realized that what I desired more than anything else was making a confession. I walked up to the front of the church to try to find a priest.

There was a button that looked like a doorbell in front of the altar with a sign: "For confessions push buzzer once."

Wow, I joked to myself, *the Church has evolved so much since I've been away. Now you can have your sins forgiven at the touch of a button!* I pushed the button and waited but no one came. I pushed it again. Still no one came, so I pushed the button a couple more times. I kept pushing the button until a small raspy voice shouted from somewhere behind a closed door, "Hold your horses! I'm coming!"

A little while later, the oldest priest I had ever seen came hobbling into the church. I could not see how he could walk so bent over without falling.

"Father," I said eagerly, "I would like to go to confession."

"Confessionals are in the back of the church," he said, looking up at me with squinty eyes.

I was worried that if we walked to the back of the church, this elderly man might die before we got there, so I told him I could do it right here.

We sat down in the front pew, and I launched into a long and drawn out confession. I had accumulated quite a list of sins in my show-business life. During the confession, I would rattle off a list of sins, and the priest would shake his head and say, "Oh, the mercy of God!"

After he gave me my penance, I asked him, "Why is the statue of Mary all decked out?"

He looked even more shocked by this than by my laundry list of sins, "You don't know what today is?"

"Father, did you just hear my confession? Of course I don't."

He shook his head again and muttered, "Oh the mercy of God! Today's the feast of the Immaculate Conception!"

After my confession, I felt a joyous relief. I was late for my rehearsal that day because I stayed for hours and prayed in the church. The next day, I went to Mass and resolved to maintain my regained spirituality. I was in love with God and was not going to turn back for anything! That lasted about two weeks.

While performing a play one Sunday, I suddenly realized I had missed Mass. That was all it took, and I went straight back to my old ways of enjoying every sin I committed. I remained in my life of sin, completely forgetting about God again.

About six months later, while walking on the Sunset Strip in Los Angeles, I heard bells ringing and saw a procession walking into a big stone cathedral. *Wow!* I thought, as I looked up at the big Gothic cathedral. Like a forgotten name abruptly remembered, the same feeling I had felt six months before returned. I walked into the cathedral. *Wow!*, I thought again. A large crowd was praying enthusiastically, amid incense, music, candles, and bells. Once again I felt a burning desire to go to confession.

On my left, I saw the confessional's red light just as it changed to green. I was afraid that the priest would leave, so I sprinted in. Then I went out into the church and prayed and prayed and prayed some more.

I was praying so fervently someone tapped me on the shoulder and asked me, "Are you a priest?"

"No," I said, "I'm just a guy who came in and didn't know what was going on. What's with all the music and bells and incense? What is today?"

"You don't know? It's the feast of the Blessed Mother!"

I stayed in that church praying until almost everyone had left. The fervor for Christ had returned, and I was determined not to let it slip away again. That lasted a few weeks. Over the next few years this happened about a dozen times. I would return to my sinful ways for months and then I would walk by a church and suddenly have an overwhelming desire to go inside and go to confession. After confession, I would remain in the church for hours and hours and hours. Then I would remain close to God for a matter of weeks before the feeling wore off. Without the feeling, I let God go.

One spring some officials at the ACT Institute of Acting, one of the best acting schools in the country, had seen a show I directed and asked me to come down to teach a seminar there in San Francisco. I was on my way to the institute, walking on Broadway near Chinatown, when I passed a little Gothic church of Saint Francis. I thought it would be good luck to go inside and say a little prayer.

The church was dark and empty. To the left, sitting on a card table, I noticed the strangest little statue I had ever seen. It was a four-foot-tall veiled statue of Mary without any hands. On a closer examination it was also covered with dark spots. *The Virgin of the Dalmatians?* I wondered. I got closer to it, and I saw that the spots were burn marks. *How strange.* My eyes scanned up to her face. Despite the damage to the rest of the statue, the glass eyes were still beautiful. I stood there for some time, staring into those eyes when I heard a voice, "Ah, so you're back again?"

I spun around to see who was there, but I saw no one. I was

embarrassed that someone was watching me since I had been just standing there staring into the eyes of a broken statue. "Who's there?" I asked, a little frightened, but it seemed that I was alone. I walked around the little church and looked everywhere. I even opened up the confessional, but I saw no one. *Maybe I imagined it. But the words were so clear.*

I returned to the statue and looked up at those eyes and mumbled, "Yeah, I guess so. I am back again." Then the voice came again like someone whispering into my ears. It said firmly: "If you do as you have done before, I will never call you back again." A realization hit me with complete clarity. I thought back to the many times I had done this before and realized that every time I entered a church with fervor to go to confession, it had been a feast of the Blessed Mother. Those beautiful glass eyes stared down at me and the words haunted me: "I will never call you back again."

I believed it was Mary who had been calling me into the church, and it was I who, after so many chances, had always ended up preferring my life of sin over God. I knelt down and prayed like I had never prayed before. I prayed fervently for forgiveness and put myself at the mercy of God. I was in love again, but this time, I was aware that I could not let that precious love ever die again.

The sound of a little Italian lady cleaning the church brought me out of prayer. I rushed to her, "Is there something I can do to help out? I just want to stay and work! I'll do anything!"

She smiled, showering her crooked little teeth, and in a thick Italian accent said, "Why, yes, we have many, many things that we need people to do."

She led me to a storage room behind the sacristy that was filled with sacred vessels, all very much in need of cleaning. "We have been wanting to take care of these," she said as she spread a white sheet over a table. She handed me a slew of rags and told me that when I was done cleaning something to put it on the sheet.

I stayed in that room cleaning for hours, carefully polishing every vessel with delicate care. Hours passed like nothing as I prayed and cleaned, cleaned and prayed. I began to hear a lot of people in the church and assumed that it must be Mass. But I did not want to be told to get out, so I kept on quietly working in the back storage room. From candle holders to tabernacles, from chalices to monstrances, everything in the room was becoming spotless. It seemed that in no time at all the church had gone silent again and the lights had been turned off. The little low-wattage bulb hanging above me was the only light left on.

When I had finished, I scanned the room for anything I had missed. I noticed a little wooden panel with a hinge on it tucked off in the corner of the room. I pried it open and inside was a little crawl space filled with dirt and ash. Using matches to see, I saw something sparkle in the black. I dug around and found that it was the point of a monstrance. I dug more and found chalices, candle holders, and countless other holy vessels all buried in dirt and singed with ash. I cleaned the dirt off of each and every one. Little by little, I was transforming filthy vessels into beautiful treasures.

As I was finishing the last candle holder, a door opened, and I heard footsteps. I looked at my watch, surprised to realize it was 1:00 a.m. *Uh-oh,* I realized. *They are going to think that I want to steal all of these expensive, holy vessels.* There I was, late at night, piling all of the vessels onto a white sheet. *Okay,* I thought, *what wouldn't a thief be doing?* I ran out into the church and knelt down to pray in front of the tabernacle. Behind me, footsteps were drawing closer and closer until they stopped right behind me. I pretended not to notice and to be praying fervently. I was tapped on the shoulder and turned to see a little Filipino priest. *Wow, if I had been robbing the church I could have flung this little guy across the room!*

"What are you doing here?" he asked, alarmed.

"There was a girl, the Italian cleaning lady, and she gave me some things to clean and so I was cleaning them…"

The priest looked surprised. "The church closed at 6:00 p.m., Do you mean you have been here since then?!"

"No, Father, I have been here since 8:00 a.m."

"Well, the church is closed. You can't be here."

The priest hurriedly led me to the door, and I left quickly, relieved to get away from this priest who had reason to be suspicious of me. The next morning, I found a priest at a different church and went to confession with the sincere desire to permanently turn my life completely over to God. I never did go to my teaching job at the ACT Institute of Acting.

After five days of prayer and attending daily Mass, I had a strong desire to return to the Church of Saint Francis to see the statue again. I slowly opened the door to the church, and there in front of the statue was the little Filipino priest praying. As the door closed behind me, the priest looked up, and I turned to get away. But the door had already closed, and my face slammed into it.

"No, no! Please! Don't run! Who are you? You cleaned things that I didn't even know existed in the church. You found the vessels that were never recovered from the fire of the Great Earthquake of 1906!"

So I sat down with the priest and told him everything. I found out that the statue of Mary had been attacked by a group of Satanists that had burned it and destroyed the hands. I was shocked to find out that it was my own mother who had ordered new hands for the statue after she read an article about it. I had not spoken to my mother in a long time. It was a coincidence beyond any odds. At the end of our long conversation, the priest agreed to be my spiritual director.

Over the next two years, my life went through an amazing transformation. I quit all acting and started living in a little rooming house next to the Church of Saint Francis. I determined that I was not ever going to leave God again. I helped out at the church in any way I could and attended daily Mass. During this time, I thought back to my childhood dream of being a priest. *No, I thought, remembering my sinful past. There's no way I could be a priest after all of the things that I have done.*

After two years without slipping back into sin, I was still uncertain about what I should do. I stopped off at the bank one day, to see how I was doing financially. With the amount of money I had, I would be set for at least another two years of indecision. On the way back from the bank on the outskirts of Chinatown, I stopped by a church called Saint Mary's. On the lectern there was a Bible sitting open. My eyes fell on the verse in Luke that says, "So therefore, no one of you can be my disciple who does not give up all his possessions ... Sell your possessions and give to charity, make yourselves purses which do not wear out, an unfailing treasure in heaven."

Since I had just come from the bank, I knew to the cent how much money was in my account. I thought about my unsure future and looked to Jesus in the tabernacle. "Okay," I prayed, "if I do this, you are going to have to take care of me from now on." I took out my checkbook. "You get me to Rome, Jesus." Slowly I wrote a check to the parish for every cent I had, and I put it into the locked collection box. I was in God's hands now.

I walked back to the house I was rooming in by the parish with a total dependence and trust in God. "I'm in your hands now," I said again and again. I arrived back at St. Francis Church, and the little Filipino priest, Father Paul, came up to me enthusiastically. "Where have you been? I've been looking for you all day!"

At the same time I was praying at Saint Mary's, a woman had visited Father Paul, and had given him an envelope. "This is for the young man who is going to Rome to study to be a priest."

"I don't know any young man going to Rome," Fr. Paul had responded, confused.

"Yes, you do," the woman said. "He's the one who reads the bingo numbers."

Inside the envelope was exactly enough money to pay for a plane ticket to Rome. It wasn't long after this, just after Christmas of 1975, that I found myself as a seminarian studying to be a priest in Rome. Every day in that seminary was an overwhelming gift for which I thanked God. It was hard to believe that I, Mr. Showbiz, was going to soon be a priest of God. To many, it may have seemed that I once lived an exciting life, but I knew that nothing was more blessed than the opportunity to serve God as a priest.

When I was ordained to the diaconate, my mother came to Rome. I asked her to consecrate me, her son, to the Blessed Mother. She smiled and said, "I already did that, long ago." Then, for the first time, she told me that when I was very young, I had come down with a high fever. When the doctor told her that I might not live, she had relinquished all of her motherly rights to the Blessed Mother. I had been dedicated to my mother in heaven, and it had been she who had directed my road to Rome to be one of her Son's priests. Suddenly, everything made perfect sense: the irresistible urges to go to confession on the feast days of the Blessed Mother, the statue, and the voice.

The Blessed Mother had kept calling me, and despite my failings, she had cleared the path to her Son and then worked tirelessly to put me on it. There were too many coincidences to doubt that my heavenly Mother had taken care of everything. Even my chalice that I had bought in a store in San Francisco bordered on the miraculous. In high school, even though I had given up hopes of becoming a priest, I had put fifty dollars down on a chalice at a Catholic store. I thought it was beautiful and just wanted it. I had never paid any more on it, but I guess the store held it for me. Years later, when I knew I would become a priest, I went looking for a chalice. I found one that looked exactly like the one I had put money down on in high school. When I went to buy it, I was informed that a priest had ordered it a year earlier. "We looked everywhere and the only store that had one like he wanted was one in Milwaukee. That's where we got it from, but the priest never came back in for it." I suddenly remembered that a year earlier my mother had wondered why some religious store had sent her a check for fifty dollars. It was the very same chalice I had wanted so many years before.

During breaks from my studies, I would put together little musical shows to perform for the rest of the seminary. After one such performance, I was told I would be performing in front of the pope! How's that for making it to the big time in showbiz? As I was singing secular songs, there was Pope John Paul II, front and center. To my relief, he seemed to be enjoying every minute of it. After the show, he embraced me and asked me my name. He thought it was hilarious when he found out I was an American. For the rest of my time in Rome, whenever he saw me, he would embrace me and exclaim in his thick Polish accent, "Ah, my American boy!"

Years later, long after I had been ordained a priest, I had brought a bagful of items I wanted to be blessed by the pope. While I waited in the packed Saint Peter's Square, he saw me and stopped his motorcade! He came over to me, remembered my name, and asked me what I was doing. I showed him all the stuff I had brought to be blessed, and to the astonished Italians looking on, the pope personally laid his hands on my stuff to bless it.

An astonished Italian woman next to me asked, "Who are you?"

I'm just a guy who came in and didn't know what was going on, I thought.

I also got the gig of being Mother Teresa's chauffeur whenever she visited the Vatican, which at that time was frequently. It was such an honor to be able to be in her presence on such a regular basis. On one occasion, I was driving her around right after I had heard that I was to be ordained by Pope John Paul II himself. Every priest who is ordained by the pope is matched up with a sister of charity so that they can be spiritual brother and spiritual sister.

As I was driving Mother around, I asked her, "Mother, is it true that I am going to be receiving a sister of charity as my spiritual sister?" She told me that was correct. I continued: "Who is your spiritual brother?"

"I don't have one," she responded.

"Don't have one?" I said. "Well, Mother, you are the head of a worldwide community, and I think you should be an example of how all things should be. So ... how about me as your spiritual brother?"

"Well, I don't know," she said. "I would have to ask the Holy Father."

"Oh, I'm just kidding, Mother," I responded, a little embarrassed. Then I all but forgot about this exchange.

Two weeks after my ordination, when I was still ecstatic about it being a done deal that I was a priest, I got a call at the seminary. "Your mother is on the phone," the seminarian told me.

"Really, my mom?"

"No, Mother Teresa," he said.

Well, I thought he was being sarcastic, but I picked up the phone. "Hello?"

The little voice on the other line said, "The Holy Father says yes. Good-bye."

Immediately, I thought someone was playing a joke on me. *Why would Mother tell me about something the Holy Father had said?* I had completely forgotten about the conversation in the car with Mother Teresa. As I was about ready to line up all 180 seminarians to ask which one of them was behind this, I remembered the conversation that I had with her in the car. I also realized that I had not told anyone about it. After all, if some people at the seminary got wind that I was asking Mother Teresa to be my spiritual sister, I might lose my post as her chauffeur. In awe, I thought: *How did the most unruly character at the seminary end up being her spiritual brother?*

I am quick to tell people that I am not a priest because of myself, but a priest in spite of myself. It was not the case that I was not enjoying my sinful life before becoming a priest; but it was not enough. Something was missing: God. I used to dream of making the "big time," not knowing that the "big time" was nothing when compared with what God had planned for me.

– Father Benjamin Francis

Since Fr. Ben's ordination, he has been something of an evangelist, traveling around Italy, the United States, Brazil, and Canada giving retreats and seminars to priests, nuns, and the clergy. He uses the same talents he once used on stage to bring others to God.

Loving the Rapist's Child

It had been more than a year since Casey was stillborn, and it seemed that Steve and I would never be able to have the third child we wanted so badly. Every passing month brought disappointment.

I sat in the doctor's waiting room, like so many times before. The nurse was used to seeing me there. She knew how hard we had tried since losing Casey. I guess that's why she just couldn't resist giving me a sly grin while practically singing her words. "The doctor will be right with you … and I think you'll like what she has to say."

The poor thing had no idea what I was really going through. The doctor came in to share my dilemma. I was pregnant all right. And neither of us was smiling. We both knew that I had been raped.

What should have been glorious news instead brought devastation of heart and memories of a brutal attack by a total stranger. Sitting there, I relived the night it happened. My husband had gone to church for a late-night meeting. I was so tired. The boys were tucked in, and I had gone to bed before Steve left. Sometime later, the light came on in our room. "Honey, turn off the light," I muttered groggily. The light went out, but there was a sense that he was just standing there in the dark, and that was annoying. I opened my eyes to see the shadowy figure of a man in the doorway. It was not my Steve.

I bolted up in bed but was promptly warned not to make a sound. Thinking of my two small sons, I complied. But the next moments were excruciating in every sense. At first I wailed, I begged; I offered to pray for the stranger who controlled my body, my life. But with a knife at my throat and threats aimed at my children, I silently endured a humiliating violation of my person. I was raped within the darkened walls of my own home—in the bed I shared with my husband.

Aloud, I asked God to forgive the man, and for a moment he stopped. I wondered whether he was feeling conviction for his sin and was going to leave me alone, or kill me. He did neither. He resumed his attack.

The trauma of rape is great. The horrifying moment grasped and exposed every hidden thing in my heart and life, from the present personal shame to deep-seated inferiority, and even the growing marital discord between Steve and me. Rape exacerbates these things and chips away at anything that is out of order or not built on solid ground.

To have my doctor tell me that I had conceived was like hearing a judge sentence me to carry a lifelong reminder of the rape. My trust in God was shaken. It's easy to chant pro-life songs when you're standing in front of an abortion clinic holding a cardboard sign. But the melody is different when you're on the other side of the poster, faced with the reality that your life is about to change dramatically—forever.

I guess that's why I took the Ovral—a pill that prevents a fertilized egg from implanting itself in the womb. It's regularly given to rape victims, quite literally to keep a potential life from taking hold.

My doctor gave me the Ovral, emphasizing the impracticality of raising a child of rape, mentioning the "just a blob of cells" line more than once. Realizing that a fertilized egg was a human embryo, I refused at first, citing that it was potentially the same as abortion. But a surprising majority of Christian friends and family members sided with the doctor. My pastor. My mother. Steve.

We were all repeatedly reminded that pregnancy was a long shot and that taking the Ovral was just a precaution to ease my mind. The case for taking the preventative was capped with reminders that the child would not look like Steve. She would be half African American.

"People will think you cheated!"

"You'll see that man's face in that child every day!"

"Do you want to tell the world you were raped? Because that's what you'll have to do."

I took the Ovral before the seventy-two-hour window had closed. Then I tried to forget about it. Of course, that was impossible with the impending fear of AIDS and the growing animosity between Steve and me.

And then, to my dismay, we discovered that the Ovral hadn't worked. I was pregnant. It seemed that my world had fallen apart, and the journey to a normal life would take a much longer time than I had thought. Perhaps I would never overcome this.

Thank God, I didn't test HIV-positive, but my doctor still advised a six-month abstinence from intimacy with Steve, until we were certain that the virus was not lurking in my body. The abstinence didn't bother me since I had no interest in intimacy, but it added to an already strained marital relationship.

We decided we should let the child be adopted and spare ourselves all the added strain of trying to love and raise a reminder of the vicious attack. We even began making arrangements with a kind couple in our church who desperately wanted a baby.

God seemed so distant, so cold. Why had he allowed me to be raped in my own home as my babies slept in the next room? And why had he allowed my third child to be conceived in this way, instead of within the sanctity of marriage, as Steve and I had planned?

But God was there. Although sin had had its run, God was there. We just had to be reminded that He is not a God of easy fixes. Steve and I became desperate, and sometimes it's that human desperation that drives us to God. We know Him; we love Him; we say we trust Him. But sometimes, we do not cleave to Him as the lover of our souls until we find ourselves completely helpless.

As for the fairness of being victimized, we have to realize that ever since sin began, there have been victims. Cain slew Abel (Gn 4:1-8). Amnon raped Tamar (2 Sm 13:1-22). But what should the victims and their families do with their pain? Do they resort to their own devices, or do they give it to God and His will?

Gradually, as the child in my body grew, both Steve and I began to change. It was a spiritual work. We grew attached to the little life inside me and delighted in its movements, just as we had marveled at the evidence of life when I carried Chad and Simon. This child was alive! It was a miracle that the child had escaped death.

It became clear that the baby was *God's* child first, and it was as innocent as those conceived any other way. We grew astonished and ashamed that we could have ever imagined not keeping the baby. We continually repented of our lack of trust in God, of putting our hand to the situation when it should have been left to God all along, and when we discovered the child was a girl, it became even more special. I particularly had wanted a daughter. The adoption was off.

When Rachael was born, a light went on in our family. We learned the true meaning of the Father's love. He looks upon us with more than acceptance. He embraces us wholeheartedly, because He has called us His children. *"For you did not receive the spirit of bondage again to fear, but you received the Spirit of adoption by whom we cry out, 'Abba, Father'"* (Rom 8:15). And in that spirit, Steve embraced Rachael as his own, and we have since adopted a wonderful older son, Deshawn.

Today, we celebrate nine wonderful years with Rachael, our only daughter. It seems like a bad dream now that we ever considered living without this amazing little girl. She is a constant reminder to us, not of rape but of the startling beauty one can find hidden in tragedy.

– Heather Gemmen Wilson

Heather Gemmen Wilson is a best-selling, award-winning author and international speaker. The preceding story was originally published in Christianity Today. *She lives in Indiana with her husband and their six children.*

One in Faith

When I first met Kris during the summer following my freshman year in college, I was immediately smitten. I was drawn to Kris as soon as I laid eyes on him at a get-together with mutual friends. He was a wrestler on a college scholarship majoring in engineering, and he worked two jobs.

On the way home, when my friends asked what I thought of him, I blurted out: "I'm going to marry him someday." Everyone laughed. I was only half joking. I did not see him again for a couple weeks. In the meantime, I let our mutual friends know that I was very interested in Kris. "He's not dating anyone right now," I was told. "He's thinking about the priesthood."

"We'll see about that," I smiled. As I look back, I cannot believe I was not running full speed in the other direction. Being from a strict Assembly of God background, I had been taught that Catholics were not Christian; they were going to hell. During high school, it was frowned upon date non-Christians or Catholics, which were one in the same as far as my family was concerned.

The reason Kris' Catholic faith did not scare me off at first was that I figured I would just set him straight. But two weeks later, when we got together with a group at the Missouri River, Kris barely noticed me. We played volleyball, and lots of girls were hanging on him. *Oh, well,* I thought to myself. *I guess I never had a chance.*

After the game, we walked over to the river. Several people suggested we swim across a narrow channel. Since it was evenly matched with guys and girls, the guys suggested they could help the girls by letting them hold onto their backs while we all swam across. Kris surprised me and offered to help me across. "No thanks," I said. "I used to be a lifeguard."

At that point, he was suddenly interested in me. For the rest of the day and late into the night, we talked. I learned that his religion was as dear to him as mine was to me. He made it clear that he would never consider any other denomination. I let him know that I was equally as adamant about my own. It seemed that things would not go any further, but a week later Kris invited me to go for a motorcycle ride. From that point on, we were inseparable. Being young and in love helped me to ignore the obvious clashes between our faiths. Instead, I saw a responsible young man who loved God and was clearly a Christian.

When August came, I returned to classes at University of Mary, while Kris transferred to finish his degree in Grand Forks at the University of North Dakota. He would be traveling a lot with the wrestling team and be busy with school. I sadly accepted that we would likely just go our separate ways. It was hard for me to accept, because other than the religious differences, Kris was everything I ever dreamed of. I tearfully said good-bye. Then I turned my attention to nursing school and tried not to think about him. To my amazement, shortly after school started up again, there was a letter from Kris. He was not forgetting me!

That Thanksgiving, I was invited to spend the holiday with Kris' family. Kris had written my dad a letter requesting permission to marry me. In spite of their anti-Catholic sentiments, they liked him. Since we were taught that one only needed to love Jesus Christ to be saved, no one could argue that Kris was not saved because he professed Jesus.

By this time, Kris and I had been talking as if marriage was inevitable, but still, I was overwhelmed by his surprise proposal. "Yes!" I gushed tearfully. "I'll marry you!" I understood intellectually what I was getting myself into. The only way to marry Kris was to get married in the Catholic Church and agree to raise our children Catholic. Together, we agreed to disagree, but I made the promise to raise our children Catholic. I figured I would keep this promise while we continued going to our own churches. Being young and so in love, it was unthinkable that anything would stand in our way.

The wedding was set for July 25, 1992. Since we were

attending college in different towns, we found a priest willing to
meet with us individually for our pre-marriage preparation. Fr.
Fahnlander planted a seed that maybe the Catholic faith was not
so bad. He told me to pray about it and said that if I was searching
for the truth, God would lead me. He gave me a book titled:
How to Survive Being Married to a Catholic. I put it aside and
soon forgot about it.

By August, we moved to Grand Forks into married housing.
I transferred to UND's nursing school, and Kris continued in
engineering and wrestling on a full scholarship. By September we
were thrilled to be expecting our first baby. Our youth elevated
our notions that we could do everything and anything. In between
my school and work and Kris' school, wrestling, and work, we
expected to have the baby and not miss a beat. Our daughter
Kaitlyn complicated things, however, when she arrived early,
during finals week. The twenty-six-hour labor and emergency
C-section dimmed my feelings of invincibility somewhat, but I
was still determined to stay the course. I took night classes so
we could take turns watching Katie, and my job at the campus
medical library allowed me to bring her to work with me.

Trying to raise a baby, work, and go to school before we had
even celebrated our first anniversary had been a lot to take on. I
was gradually wearing out. When Katie was baptized a couple
weeks after her birth, reality bore down on me. In my church,
babies are dedicated to God. Baptism does not take place until
much later when a person feels ready to commit his life to God.
Watching my baby girl take part in a ceremony I did not agree
with made me feel alone and sad. *Was it a mistake to promise to
raise my children Catholic?* I wondered. *What if my family was right
and my daughter was not really going to be Christian?*

That year I sometimes feared that maybe Catholics were
not really Christians after all. Little by little, the reality of the
lifetime commitment I had made began to scare me. Every night,
Kris would pray the Rosary and invite me to join him. Since I

had been taught that praying to Mary was idolatry and would send a person to hell, I always declined and left the room. Kris brought home piles of Catholic books for me to read, but I was not interested. This frustrated him. Our first St. Valentine's Day together, we had a huge argument over this issue. *What did I get myself into?* I cried. After the argument, Kris talked to a priest. He told Kris that the seeds were planted and now he needed to just pray—no more piles of books and no more arguments.

Then, when Katie was two months old, I began to feel extra tired and thought I had picked up the flu. When the symptoms hung on, I realized that I was pregnant again. Now, it was clear I could not continue in nursing school. Within a couple more months, Katie was getting too big for me to bring into work anymore, so I quit. Life was crumbling all around me, and I did not even have God to hang onto. I was not going to my church and felt spiritually disconnected when I went with Kris to his. I had stopped reading the Bible and felt empty inside. Since everyone around me was single, I had no friends to whom I could relate, so I became a hermit. Then things got worse.

I delayed seeing a doctor until I was almost five months along. Since my doctor was still doing his residency, he had another doctor overseeing him. My previous C-section and getting pregnant again so soon made me high risk, so I needed to consult with the supervising physician.

Looking at the ultrasound pictures and then at me, a severe look of irritation clouded the doctor's face. "You got pregnant when your baby was only two months old and you were not even healed," she said angrily. "If you try to carry this baby to term, you and the baby have a strong chance of both dying. Your uterus could rupture." Then, very matter-of-factly, she told me to terminate the pregnancy. I was dumbfounded. Shaking with fear and anger and without uttering a word, I left the office. The doctor's advice infuriated me. She was supposed to take care of me, but instead she was telling me to kill my baby. I told the resident doctor that I did not want her anywhere near me. He apologized and said I could have my prenatal appointments with him but she would have to do the actual C-section.

When I told Kris, he shared my outrage. In spite of our spiritual differences, we still shared core values. Kris realized that I was depressed, so he tried his best to cheer me up, but between his school, a part-time job, studying, and traveling with the wrestling team, I was alone with the baby most of the time. Out of boredom, I started reading some of the religion books Kris had around the apartment. I even came across the book Fr. Fahnlander had given to me during our engagement. It explained the seven sacraments and gave biblical references. I longed to be connected to God again, so I also began praying and reading my Bible again. Little by little, the Catholic faith started to make sense to me. I still struggled, however, with the sacrament of confession and praying to Mary. After talking to a priest at the Newman Center who explained that God is the one forgiving sins and the priest is merely standing in for him, I began to understand confession. I did not want Kris to pressure me or get his hopes up, so I kept all this to myself. There was still one major hurdle I could not get over—Mary. I longed to be completely one with Kris, but I could not fully share his faith if it meant idolatry.

I understood that Catholics ask Mary to take their intentions to her Son, Jesus, who is the one they worship, but years of having it impressed upon me that this was idolatry, blocked me from accepting a devotion to Mary.

I was raised with the idea of putting out a fleece. (Gideon does this in Judges 6:36-40 as a way of asking for a sign. Whether or not there was dew on the fleece in the morning determined his answer from God.) So I said: "OK, Lord, I want you to send me an unmistakable sign that could only come from you, that this Catholic devotion to Mary is right and that the Catholic religion is the true faith." If he sent me that sign, I would become Catholic.

Two weeks before my due date, I began praying this daily.

Instead of another long labor, the scheduled C-section would be more predictable. I was given an epidural in the delivery room. While lying on the table after the epidural, I suddenly felt very sick. Darkness clouded my brain as if I was on the verge of losing consciousness, and there was ringing in my ears. I gasped for breath, but it felt like a two-hundred-pound weight was crushing my lungs. Everyone was busy around the room, not noticing my crisis. Suddenly, my mind flashed back to the doctor's dire prediction that both the baby and I would likely die.

I tried to tell someone that I could not breathe, but no words came out. The only thing that came was tears. One of the student nurses, Risa, a friend from nursing school, noticed me crying. I finally expressed to her that I could not breathe. My heart rate skyrocketed, and the monitors started going crazy. This is it, I thought. I'm dying. All of a sudden, I started praying the Rosary. One mystery after another, I knew them and prayed out loud. Kris entered the room after washing up and putting on a gown. I had an oxygen mask on by then. He could tell I was praying, but did not realize it was the Rosary.

Once I started praying the Rosary, a restful calm surged through me and vanquished all fear. The tears kept streaming, but now they were tears of joy. It was my sign! I had never learned how to pray the Rosary! I never read about it or listened to one being prayed. I always left the room when Kris or his family began the Rosary. But suddenly, as if through a divine infusion, I knew each mystery from the joyful, sorrowful, and glorious mysteries, just as they are taken from the life of Jesus in the Gospel.

My spirit soared! God had answered my prayers and let me know that I could become Catholic. It was okay to honor Our Blessed Mother and ask for her intercession. As my second baby daughter, Alexandria (Ali), was lifted up for me to see, I was giddy with excitement and joy. Ali, my little girl, was joining a family that would be completely one. Nothing could take away my complete happiness; not even the mean doctor who warned

Kris after sewing up my incision: "You had better take care of this or you are going to have a dead wife on your hands." All fear of the future was replaced with a sureness of faith.

Again, I kept this from Kris. For now, the excitement of our new baby was enough for him. My experience was so intense and so personal, I was not yet ready to share it. I needed time to process everything.

A month after Ali was born, Kris and I found a trailer to buy in Bismarck, where he began working with the family company. After spending a couple of nights in our new home, on Saturday morning I felt it was time to tell Kris. "Well," I began, "I'm ready to convert."

"Convert to what?" he asked, confused.

"To the Catholic Church," I answered.

His eyes opened wide. "That's not funny," he said, warily.

When I reassured him that I was totally serious, he leaped out of bed in his boxer shorts. "Yahoo!" he yelled and danced around the trailer. Then he called his mom to share his excitement. A couple days later, I began classes to prepare to join the Catholic Church. This time, when Ali was baptized, instead of feeling alone, I looked down at the baptismal waters that brought her into the Church and I thought, soon it will be me.

On April 15, 1995, three days before Ali's first birthday, I was confirmed and welcomed into the Catholic Church. Kris bought me a new diamond for my wedding ring and we had it blessed to mark this occasion. When we look back, Kris and I still sit dumbfounded that we ever gave each other a chance but now, we thank God that we did.

— Rebecca Lengenfelder

Rebecca Lengenfelder lives in Bismarck, North Dakota, with her husband and five (soon to be six) children. She keeps busy homeschooling their children and is also the confirmation director in her parish.

Chapter 3

He Picked Me Up When I Was Down

All Is Forgiven, Sadie Hawkins!

When I was in high school, every February saw the annual ritual of Sadie Hawkins Day. Sadie Hawkins was a character in the old cartoon strip *Li'l Abner* who took things into her own hands when it came to "datin'," "courtin'," and all the rest of the male-female frou-frou that so occupies the adolescent mind. Sadie didn't wait for a guy to ask her out; she asked him.

So, once a year, in honor of dear Sadie, my alma mater held a dance in which the girls asked the guys out for a change. The net result of this arrangement was to create a social situation in which a small but stable group of insecure boys were reminded for four years straight that no girl in the school would touch them with a barge pole. Your on-the-scene correspondent is here to tell you that this is but one of the reasons Graduation Day 1976 was a tremendous relief to me. It is also the reason that February, for many years, triggered in me a deep and abiding gloom. To a non-Christian like me, it was the least worthwhile month in the calendar. Christmas was dead and gone, while dark winter still hung around. After President's Day, there wasn't going to be another holiday till spring break. Homework was only going to increase. And here was the Marquis de Sadie, putting up posters all over the school to remind you that, on top of everything else, pretty much everybody in the world—except for you—was lovable and fascinating to *some*body.

In high school, I profoundly believed in my unique social leprosy, and in my utter failure to be part of the "in crowd." On my worst days, I congratulated myself that this uniqueness was due to my vast intellectual superiority over the masses who just could not understand me. On my next worst days, I swung to the opposite pole and accounted for my sense of unique isolation by accusing myself of being one whom my fellow human beings could not be expected to tolerate for long.

What never occurred to me in high school was that I was not unique at all and that the great mass of my fellow human beings felt as isolated, klutzy, stupid, and unlovable as I did. I was so fretful about getting "in" that it never occurred to me that, a) most people were as "out" as I was and, b) "in" was not all that worth getting.

It was our Lord, in his Catholic Church, who began to heal this terrible sense of being outcast. For our Lord is, if anything, the center of all things. He is as "in" as you can get, the heart of all life, the center of all being, the very fountainhead of existence. And yet, right here, I found a paradox. For the Son of Man is cast out by men. More than that, He deliberately turns His back on all the social climbing, cliques, and posturing that so occupied my high school mind (and continues to occupy the more sophisticated high school lunchrooms known as Hollywood, Washington, D.C., and New York). When the Sinmeister offered Him chance to be *People* magazine's Most Fascinating Person of A.D. 30 ("All this will I give you," said Satan, "if you will bow down and worship me."), our Lord chose the obscurity and ostracism I so feared. When offered all the kingdoms of the world, He opted for the desert. Why? Because He knew that at the center of this dog-eat-dog world there is no "there" there. He came, not to get in, but to get *us*. Where I was so sweaty about making something of myself in order to finally be lovable, He had long ago made nothing of Himself—because He loved us.

– Mark P. Shea

Mark P. Shea is a popular writer and speaker. In addition to being co-author of the bestseller A Guide to the Passion: 100 Questions about The Passion of the Christ, *he is also the author of* The Da Vinci Deception: 100 Questions about the Facts and Fiction of the Da Vinci Code, Making Senses Out of Scripture: Reading the Bible as the First Christians Did, By What Authority?: An Evangelical Discovers Catholic Tradition, *and* This is My Body: An Evangelical Discovers the Real Presence. *His column "Connecting the Dots" appears in the* National Catholic Register. *Mark is also Senior Content Editor for CatholicExchange.com. He lives in Washington state with his wife, Janet, and their four sons.*

Survivors' Wisdom

We are like teabags whose strength comes out when we're put in hot water. So, when problems upset you ... just think, you must be God's favorite cup of tea!

— *Unknown*

Extraordinary afflictions are not always the punishment of extraordinary sins, but sometimes the trial of extraordinary graces.

— *Matthew Henry*

God wastes nothing—not even sin. The soul that has struggled and come through is enriched by its experiences, and Grace does not merely blot out the evil past but in the most literal sense "makes it good."

— *Dorothy Sayers*

Strength and courage aren't always measured in medals and victories. They are measured in the struggles they overcome. The strongest people aren't always the people who win, but the people who don't give up when they lose.

— *Ashley Hodgeson*

I know God won't give me anything I can't handle. I just wish he didn't trust me so much.

— *Blessed Teresa of Calcutta*

Don't let life discourage you. Everyone who got where he is had to begin where he was.

— *Richard L. Evans*

Don't get upset with your imperfections. It's a great mistake because it leads nowhere—to get angry because you are angry, upset at being upset, depressed at being depressed, disappointed because you are disappointed. So don't fool yourself. Simply surrender to the Power of God's Love, which is always greater than our weakness.

> *— St. Francis de Sales*

Grace flows through wounds.

> *— Christopher West*

Yield thou not to adversity, but press on the more bravely.
> *— Virgil*

Do everything calmly and peacefully. Do as much as you can as well as you can. Strive to see God in all things without exception, and consent to His will joyously. Do everything for God, uniting yourself to Him in word and deed. Walk very simply with the Cross of the Lord and be at peace with yourself.

> *— St. Francis de Sales*

No one, however weak, is denied a share in the victory of the cross. No one is beyond the help of the prayer of Christ.

> *— St. Leo the Great*

Pray, hope, and don't worry.

> *— St. Pio of Pietrelcina*

Now it is our turn; and all ministering spirits keep silence and look on. Oh let not your foot slip, or your eye be false, or your ear dull, or your attention flagging! Be not dispirited; be not afraid; keep a good heart; be bold; draw not back; you will be carried through ... Oh children of a heavenly Father, be not afraid!

> *— John Henry Cardinal Newman*

Above the clouds the sky is always blue.
— *St. Thérèse of Lisieux*

We are not the sum of our weaknesses and failures, we are the sum of the Father's love for us and our real capacity to become the image of His Son Jesus.
— *Pope John Paul II*

"The times are bad! The times are troublesome!" This is what humans say. But we are our times. Let us live well and our times will be good. Such as we are, such are our times.
— *St. Augustine*

Anxiety does not empty tomorrow of its sorrows but only empties today of its strength.
— *Unknown*

We are uncertain of the next step, but we are certain of God. Immediately we abandon to God, and do the duty that lies nearest, and He packs our life with surprises all the time... Leave the whole thing to Him. It is gloriously uncertain how He will come in, but He will come.
— *Oswald Chambers*

Unfurl the sails, and let God steer us where He will.
— *St. Bede*

The great danger for most of us is not that our aim is too high and we miss it, but that it is too low and we reach it.
— *Michelangelo*

First do what is necessary, then do what is possible, and before long you will find yourself doing the impossible.
— *St. Francis of Assisi*

Have courage for the great sorrows of life and patience for the small ones; and when you have laboriously accomplished your daily task, go to sleep in peace. God is awake.
— Victor Hugo

I believe that nothing that happens to me is meaningless, and that it is good for us all that it should be so, even if it runs counter to our own wishes. As I see it, I'm here for some purpose and I only hope I may fulfill it. In the light of the great purpose all our privations and disappointments are trivial.
— Dietrich Bonhoeffer

When life knocks you to your knees, you are in the perfect position to pray.
— Anonymous

Marriage Marathon

Elizabeth waited for her husband Jim's face to crack with a smile so that she could tell him that these sorts of jokes were not funny. But it was no joke. "What do you mean? You've always believed in marriage as a holy sacrament. How can you just walk out and leave us?" He told her that he had never loved her and that they never should have married. With that he packed his things, and life as Elizabeth had known it took an irrevocable turn down a road she never would have imagined embarking upon.

Though their marriage had had its strains recently, Elizabeth thought that their newest baby would bring them closer together. Now she found herself a single parent responsible for two active children and a newborn.

After the initial shock came lonely days of wondering what had gone wrong and how to handle the future. She needed to find full-time work to support her three children and was forced for a time to move into her parents' basement.

While Elizabeth struggled, she managed to keep her joyous optimism and believed that God would carry her through. Her ex-husband initiated an annulment process as the Church investigated to find out if the marriage had been a sacramental one. After a time, Elizabeth found the peace of mind to accept whatever outcome God had in store for her. If that meant remaining single for the rest of her life, so be it.

Elizabeth's struggle was similar to one that a man named John was facing on his own. He had been married for twelve years and had two small children. He watched as his wife Jane began replacing Sunday morning church with a part-time job. As her co-workers slowly began to replace her family and friends, John realized that she no longer loved him.

Two-and-a-half years later, John found himself ordered to leave his home. He found a two-bedroom apartment near his children's school so that he could remain a big part of their lives.

During the first three years on his own, through the pain, he felt God's presence in his life and stayed faithful to Him. Despite a good job, John found it hard to pay for spousal maintenance, child support, and legal bills. Notwithstanding these struggles, John felt that at least he and his children were enjoying life again.

Through her struggles as a single parent, Elizabeth had finally saved enough money to make a down payment on a home. Her friend Jill invited her to dinner with her and her husband to celebrate. She casually mentioned, "We have a neighbor we'd like to invite along as well."

Elizabeth, sensing this was a set-up countered, "What is this? A blind date? I'm not sure about it."

Jill reassured her. "He's perfect. He and Tom are running buddies and we've known him for years. He has two children who live next door to us with their mother."

"So he's divorced, too?"

"Yes. His situation is similar to yours in that he didn't want the divorce. He has been living on his own for several years. He's one of the nicest men I've ever met and a terrific father to his children! Come on, Elizabeth. Would you please? If nothing else, just go out for dinner." Elizabeth agreed to give it a try.

While picking out her dress for the occasion, Elizabeth felt the distantly familiar feeling of butterflies she had not experienced in a long time.

The evening ended up being enjoyable for everyone. Jill and Tom were as surprised as Elizabeth and John that both had ordered the same meal. They thought to themselves, "Who could order such an odd combination and not be meant for each other?"

As Elizabeth waited anxiously to see if John would call her again, John had already called Tom to ask, "Is it too soon to call her again? I can't stop thinking about her. I don't want to scare her off. She's almost too good to be true."

Tom reassured him. "Elizabeth is genuine. We've known her a long time. She wasn't putting on a show for you; that's just how wonderful she is all the time. Go ahead! Give her a call. She'd love it!"

Over the next nine months, Elizabeth and John went out often. He mustered up enough courage to ask if he could hold her hand. It was nine months later before he asked for his first kiss goodnight. Elizabeth giggled and said, "I can't believe you asked for permission to kiss me!"

When Elizabeth won a contest that allotted a large sum to be used for travel, she signed up to go on a trip to the Holy Land with a tour group of friends from her church. She invited a close girlfriend to go as her roommate and also invited John. Ever since he had met Elizabeth, John had been intrigued with the Catholic faith and thought a Catholic tour of the Holy Land was a great opportunity to explore it further.

In the Holy Land, both prayed together that God's will be done in them. They strengthened their relationship through frequent prayer and put God in the center.

After the tour, John enrolled in the RCIA (Rite of Christian Initiation for Adults) classes at Elizabeth's church, and on Easter he received confirmation and Holy Eucharist with Elizabeth as his sponsor.

John realized that if he wanted to live the rest of his life with Elizabeth, he would need to get an annulment, and so he started the long process to obtain one. Elizabeth had already received an annulment on her marriage.

What if his marriage isn't annulled? Elizabeth wondered often. *I am almost on the verge of putting my life back together. If John can't be part of my life permanently, what will I do? I can't turn my back on the Church, but the more I know of John, the less I think I can go through life without him.* Painful as that thought was, both Elizabeth and John were determined to follow the Church, whatever the result would be.

After delays, a pronouncement was made. John was about to leave on a business trip when he called Elizabeth. "I got the notice, but I don't want to open it without you. I am about to leave for the airport, and I'll be gone three days! What can we do?"

"I'll meet you at your house!" Elizabeth exclaimed as she hurried out her door.

Their matchmaker friend Tom met them at John's house. Tom prayed over John and Elizabeth and their hope for marriage. Then John and Elizabeth prayed together and said, "God, your will be done." With shaking hands, John tore open the announcement. "It's annulled," he said in amazement. Elizabeth's bright eyes were flooded with tears. They thanked God for His blessing.

Not long after the pronouncement, John went over to Elizabeth's house after work and asked to make her dinner. John had made a CD of twenty love songs telling Elizabeth how much he loved her and how he wanted to spend the rest of his life with her. He asked Elizabeth to sit on the couch and they listened to all twenty of the songs and then John got down on one knee and said, "That's how I feel about you. Will you marry me?" He reached in the seat cushion and grabbed the ring that had been planted there earlier. Elizabeth said yes, and they danced together in the living room, listening to the songs once more. Instead of cooking dinner, John had a surprise party set up for Elizabeth at their favorite restaurant with several friends waiting to help celebrate.

At the wedding, people came and experienced the beginning of a joyful future that few expected, given the couple's previous trials. Their children were present as they all prayed that their family would be a witness to others of God's hope and His love.

As the guests gathered at the reception, John and Elizabeth exchanged gifts. John lovingly washed Elizabeth's feet and told her that he wanted to be like Jesus: a true servant. Elizabeth's gift to John was a promise to train with him for an upcoming marathon, which they would run together. She kept her promise, and they crossed the finish line holding hands, signifying that they were in the race together for the long haul.

While it seems to an outsider that a marathon is run on the

day of the race, any marathon runner will tell you otherwise. A marathon, like a marriage, is hardly about the wedding day or the day of the race. It is about the countless little feats leading up to it. It is about the months of work, preparation, and faith that it can be done. To Elizabeth and John, a marathon, and the months of work and dedication to complete it, pale in comparison to the struggles they overcame that led to their wedding. And until the race is over, they have committed to run it together under the watchful eye of their personal trainer, God.

– Luke Armstrong

Luke Armstrong is a co-editor of Amazing Grace for Survivors. *His biography appears at the end of the book.*

Note: *Names have been changed in this story to protect the couple's privacy.*

Mary, the Mother Who Waits — Part One

Why go to Jesus' mother when I could go directly to the Source of answered prayer? My relationship with God had always been a high priority. I wasn't afraid of Him, and I knew that He heard me. I did from time to time ask my friends to pray for me when things got tough, but that was different (or so I thought). The very idea of talking to Jesus' mother held no appeal.

In the years that followed my conversion to Catholicism, slowly my outlook began to change. It all began with a romantic disappointment, which left me dreading going to Mass alone (my friend and I had always gone together). I mentioned this to "Marilyn," a mature Catholic friend, and her response floored me. "Have you told Mary about it?" I shook my head. "Why would I do that?" "She's your mother, too, you know. She cares." Opening her purse, Marilyn took out a little metal disk imprinted with an image of Mary and the infant Jesus. A blue piece of yarn was strung through it to form a necklace.

"Here. Take this. The next time you feel lonely, ask Mary to help you." Not seeing a graceful way to get out of it, I accepted her gift. I put the medal on the passenger seat of my car and promptly forgot about it.

That Sunday, my eyes fell on the medal as I drove into the church parking lot. Almost gingerly, I picked it up. It was still cold with winter chill. Closing my eyes, I said, "God, I don't know if I should be doing this. If this isn't something I should be doing, don't let anything happen today that I could take as a sign that this is OK." I paused, then took a breath and spouted out, "Mary-if-you-can-hear-me-I'd-like-someone-to-sit-with-in-church-today-Amen." I entered the church, went to my usual pew, piled my coat and purse beside me (on the aisle, so no one could slip in while I wasn't looking), got down on the kneeler, and began to pray.

When the pastor told us to turn and greet people, I looked up to find a woman about my age standing next to me. "Hi! Can I sit with you? I just moved here a month ago and don't know anyone yet." Dumbfounded, I moved my coat and let her slide in.

It's a fluke, I told myself.

The next week, I repeated the same routine, asking God to keep me from error, sending up a quick reminder to Mary that I wanted someone to sit with, and then going into the church and barricading myself in the pew. When I looked up that time, an older woman was standing there. "Can I sit with you, dear?" The third week I knew what was going to happen. "I mean it, God. I'm going to keep doing this if You keep sending me pew mates. Mary, I'd like someone to sit with me. Amen." That week I had not one but four companions ... a new family had settled in front of me, displacing the four Hispanic sisters who usually occupied that row. One of them, Anna, tapped me on the shoulder. "Would you mind letting us sit with you this week?" OK, God. Got it. From that point on, I knew that when things got ugly, I always had someone who would look out for me as only a mother could.

But Mary was not giving me preferential treatment. Years later, in line at the seminary cafeteria before class one day, I noticed a woman behind me was carrying a copy of a book I had written about Mary. I asked her if she'd like me to sign the book for her. She looked at me as if I'd just slapped her.

"What's wrong?" I asked.

"You wrote this? Really?" I nodded, smiling. Haltingly, she said, "It's just that ... well, I read about how you asked Mary to send someone to sit with you in church. I asked her to send someone to sit with me at lunch today. And she did ... the author of this book!"

– Heidi Hess Saxton

Heidi Hess Saxton converted to the Catholic faith in 1994. She and her husband, Craig, adopted their two foster children in 2005, and live in southern Michigan. For more information about Heidi and her books, go to her parenting blog http:// mommymonsters.blogspot.com.

The preceding story originally appeared in Behold Your Mother: Mary Stories and Reflections of a Catholic Convert, *by Heidi Hess Saxton. To read more Mary stories, go to http://beholdyourmotherbook.blogspot.com. To order a copy of Heidi's book, go to www.christianword.com*

Stay and Be Light

In our early twenties, my wife and I finally gave way to a fallen-away Catholic's invitation to a Sunday morning Baptist service. It turned out to be a moving experience. That one hour seemed to highlight for me all the dysfunction in my Catholic parish that was seething beneath the surface of my heart. The cold environment, the poor homilies, the dreary music, the lack of zeal for God. I turned to my wife and said, "We should start coming here. Maybe we can slip into a Catholic Church on Monday for the Eucharist."

That night I was brushing my teeth when I suddenly heard clearly in my heart the words, *"Stay and be light to your brothers."* I stopped, and heard them again. *"Stay and be light to your brothers."* I told my wife, Lea, what had happened, and she agreed: we should stay in the Catholic Church.

A short time later, my mom sat me down in a chair to watch a video in which an ex-Protestant pastor explained how he had set out to debunk the Catholic Church. In the course of his historical and theological study, he found that what the Church teaches has been consistent through the centuries, back to the apostles. Dr. Scott Hahn converted and became a Catholic, eventually taking thousands of Protestants with him. By the end of the video, I had tears streaming down my face. My heart suddenly burned with a deep love for the Church because it was Jesus' Church, the one He built on Peter the Rock.

I spent the next two years pouring over the teachings of the Church until one day I received another word from the Lord: *"Music is a doorway to evangelize."* With that, I began a Catholic praise and worship band that met monthly. After four years, there were up to seven or eight hundred Catholics worshipping with us on a Sunday night as we'd preach the Gospel and then lead them through song into a personal encounter with Jesus. It was powerful.

After those four years, several of us branched off into our own ministries, many of which are still growing to this day and evangelizing the Church.

During the Jubilee Year 2000, I had just consecrated my ministry to Our Lady of Guadalupe. I was asked to come to a Canadian bishop's diocese to bring a vision for evangelization. It was a vision that melded the preaching of the Gospel with Eucharistic adoration, "baptism of the Holy Spirit," and basic apologetics. I felt there would be an explosion of graces for those to whom we ministered.

Instead, we hit a stone-cold wall of apathy. The clergy were not interested in lay ministry, and the majority of the people to whom we were sent were not interested in being ministered to outside of the Sunday Mass. After six months, only the bishop's support remained. Soon the financial strain on the diocese would put an end to that support.

I looked at my wife sitting across the living room, pregnant with our fifth child, and threw my arms up into the air. "That's it! Let's kick the dust off our sandals and go home." The problem was, we had no home. We had left everything to come to the Okanagan Valley, one of Canada's prettiest and wealthiest regions, a garden of Eden.

We began the fourteen-hour journey through the mountains back to the prairies. We finally arrived the next day at Lea's parents' farm. I stood outside the vehicle and gaped at the barren landscape. The snow was gone, but there was no sign of life. And my heart was an utter desert. I felt as though I had been kicked out of the Garden of Eden.

As we unloaded our belongings into the garage and moved our family into some spare rooms, the feeling that I was an utter failure began to sink in. I had thirsted to serve God in ministry for nearly ten years. But now I was broken, my desire given over to resignation. I picked up my guitar one last time and put it in its case, vowing out loud, "Lord, I will never pick up this guitar for ministry every again." I paused and added, "Unless you ask me to."

With that I turned my heart toward the marketplace, resolving to quietly live the Gospel in the workforce, minding my own business, providing for my family until I was old and gray.

The problem was, I couldn't find any work.

We talked about farming, but the future in that was even bleaker. The only job that presented itself after weeks of searching was selling a little square of advertising on a diner paper placemat to local businesses. I took the job. But after spending the first day giving it my best shot, only one out of all the businesses I approached seemed remotely interested. We would starve at this rate!

I was humiliated. Only a few short years ago, I had been an award-winning television reporter with a major Canadian television station. Now I was scraping the bottom of the barrel. And even that had rusted out.

The next day, I took one of my many long walks down the road, praying the Rosary, talking out loud to God. During the past four months since leaving the Valley, it seemed as though He had abandoned me. My prayers would leave my lips and seemingly be carried away by the prairie wind into nothingness. It was as though He had left me, or worse yet, was punishing me. I had failed Him, and He had moved on. Sometimes a small voice would say that He did not exist and that I was a random product of the universe, no different from last year's leaves blowing across the dry pastures.

But I clung to my rosary and walked deeper into the darkness of faith, the blackness hemming me in. One evening as I sat on a bale and watched the sun set, I finally cried out to God. "Lord, *please*, I am buying diapers on my credit card. How can this be Your will? Please, help us." My dignity as a man had been crushed into a powder. Or rather, the image of who I thought I was had been shattered, and I was left standing naked before the bitter reality of my humanity and my sheer poverty.

I started walking back to the farm. It was a long road that went on for miles and miles, as far as the eye could see. When I got to the driveway, for the first time in months, I suddenly heard the Lord speak in my heart. "Will you keep going?" I looked down the road. I thought of my babies and pregnant wife in the farmhouse. And I heard it again. "Will you keep going?"

"Yes, Lord."

I stood there and waited for a directive. There was nothing but the sound of the wind passing through the budding trees.

The next day, the phone rang. It was for me. "It's Alan— your old boss," my wife whispered. We exchanged puzzled looks. Hardly a soul knew where we were. Twenty minutes later, the call ended. I turned to my wife. "I've been offered a job to host and produce my own television show."

A year later, I was sitting in an executive office, the ratings on my show climbing, driving a company SUV to work, managing three employees, and making the best salary I had ever made. But as I stared at the country view outside my window, I couldn't understand why I felt restless. "Don't I have everything a guy could want?" But something else was happening *with my music*.

I was asked to sing at a few churches that month. I said to myself, "I'm not going to do any ministry. I'll sing my love songs. God can speak through that." But when I gave the concerts, a "word" would begin to burn in my heart, and I would end up preaching in between some of the songs. Afterward, people would approach me and say, "I enjoyed your music, but *what you said* really ministered to my heart." Later, I would speak to the Lord and say, "I promised I would not do any ministry, Lord. I'll stick to singing my love songs." But then, the next concert, the same thing would happen. My heart would burn with a message. It became clear to me that God had something to say, and for some reason, He wanted to use me as His "little courier." How could I deny what was happening in the hearts of those who came to listen?

One of the messages that burned in my heart was the terrible silence over abortion in Canada. And so, one day at home, I penned a letter to the newspapers criticizing us "journalists" for being willing to cover every graphic murder, domestic violent crime, or war scene, but refusing to publish the pictures that clearly showed the reality of abortion. I signed my name as a producer of the TV station I worked for.

The backlash was immediate. The newspaper chains wanted to do follow-up stories, but only to sensationalize my stance, not to address the issue. My company warned me that to say anything more would put me in jeopardy. Memos were fired off, some sent to the entire news staff attacking my position and me.

A month later, I was laid off, and my show was cut. The station managers insisted it had nothing to do with my letter. As I stood looking out upon the familiar landscape of unemployment, I turned to my wife and said; "There's nothing for me to do now *but* ministry." This time, there was a tremendous peace. Still, how on earth was I to support a family? But what mattered was God's will. This time, a burning desire for ministry was replaced with fear and trembling. I understood St. Paul's words to the Colossians very well.

Like Abraham who was about to sacrifice his son, Isaac, upon an altar, the Lord asked me to place upon the altar not only my music but my desire to serve Him. It made no more sense than it had to Abraham, who, after many years without children, was given Isaac—and told to give him back. But at the last second, when God saw that Abraham was willing to obey, the Lord provided a ram to sacrifice instead. The Lord was not punishing me. Rather, He wanted the ministry to be in, of, and through Him. It's about Him, not me.

Since my secular work has ended, my ministry has grown to extraordinary measure. My wife and I have traveled to three different continents and ministered to tens of thousands of souls. My ministry includes concerts, parish missions, and school evangelization. More recently, I've returned to my roots of leading people into an "encounter with Jesus," but this time, through Eucharistic Adoration. In all these years of ministry, *we've never missed a meal.* We have since been richly blessed with three more healthy children, with one more on the way. More importantly, we've learned through the trials and crosses that come with serving the Lord (Sir 2:1), that He will never, ever abandon us.

– Mark Mallett

Mark Mallett began singing and playing the guitar at the age of nine and went on to become an award-winning television journalist. Mark is now a full-time singer-songwriter and Catholic evangelist. He tours extensively throughout North America and abroad, singing and speaking in churches and schools. In 2006, Mark was a guest on EWTN and had the privilege of singing at the Vatican and presenting his music to Pope Benedict XVI. Together with his wife, Lea, Mark has eight beautiful children and makes his home in western Canada. You can visit his website at www.markmallett.com.

Bald and Beautiful

When Caitlin Riley arrived on the campus of Kalamazoo College to begin her freshman year, she was one new student who got noticed. She's smart, so her professors certainly noticed her abilities and enjoyed having Caitlin in class. She's friendly, so the girls in her dorm probably appreciated her sense of humor and willingness to listen. She's beautiful, so the guys on campus must have noticed her sparkling smile and expressive eyes.

Of course, those traits were not the first thing people noticed. Ever since she stopped wearing a wig, the first thing people notice is her baldness. Yet, once people get past her unique appearance, the thing everyone discovers is Caitlin's amazing outlook on life.

Caitlin suffers from alopecia areata, an incurable auto-immune disorder that struck when she was only twelve. Alopecia attacks the hair follicles and can cause patchy hair loss or complete baldness. It can be temporary or permanent and can strike repeatedly. More than five million Americans suffer from alopecia, the cause of which is not known.

In Caitlin's case, alopecia caused her hair to fall out in patches. It began at a particularly difficult time of life: seventh grade. By her freshman year at Lansing Catholic Central High School, Caitlin had lost enough hair to receive a wig through the Locks of Love program. Instead of the concerns that typically consume the thoughts of a teenage girl, Caitlin was faced with finding a wig that would make her look "normal."

"At first I prayed that it would stop," she recalls. But she thought God didn't answer her prayers, so Caitlin gave up. "After a while, I didn't pray at all." Caitlin blamed God for putting her through such a harrowing experience, and she held a grudge for a long time.

At the same time, Caitlin hid her baldness. "I played soccer, so that was challenging," she says. "I didn't really put myself out there on the field because I was always worried about my wig moving around." Once, in a high-school soccer game, the wig slipped back without her realizing how much of her head it had revealed. "No one said anything," Caitlin says, "but it was really embarrassing."

Caitlin always wore her wig in public; at home with her parents, Laura and Tom, she felt comfortable without it. "Only a few of my closest friends knew I was bald, and I would sometimes go without the wig if we were hanging around my house, but I never went anywhere without wearing it." The wig hid her baldness, but it also hid her playfulness, her spontaneity, and her spirit. "I just didn't feel like I was really me," she says of this time in her life.

A little more than a year ago, God seemed finally to answer Caitlin's prayers, though not in a way she had expected. It all started in her junior year when Caitlin began a friendship with Pamela Haan, the mother of one of Caitlin's classmates. Caitlin had seen Pam around school wearing a scarf or a hat, seemingly unself-conscious about being bald. Wondering if they had alopecia in common, Caitlin approached her, only to learn that Pam's baldness was caused by chemotherapy. But seeing Pam at Ash Wednesday Mass stirred Caitlin and inspired her. She admired the courage and peace she saw in Pam and decided it was time to come to terms with alopecia.

In the summer of 2005, Caitlin attended a conference for alopecia sufferers. The conference found Caitlin among hundreds of men, women, and children who shared her condition, many of whom comfortably displayed their baldness. "It was amazing to be around all these people without wigs," she recalls. Being among others with alopecia gave Caitlin the courage to take her wig off, too. "It felt great! It was liberating," she says.

After the first day of the conference, her wig stayed in the hotel room while Caitlin explored the limits of her newfound freedom. She even went swimming for the first time in more than five years. Finally, Caitlin felt like herself again. She made the decision to stop wearing a wig. Facing the prospect of starting her senior year at Lansing Catholic Central High School with a whole new persona, Caitlin decided to share her story with the school community. She wrote a letter to parents and students before the school year began to let people know that her baldness was caused by a disease and that she would be attending school without a wig. She did not want people to wonder about her, and she hoped to avoid any teasing or taunts. On the first day of the 2005-2006 academic year, Caitlin was the featured speaker at the school's opening assembly. Standing alone and bald with more than five hundred of her peers watching, she told her story—a remarkable journey of faith and courage. Her schoolmates responded with a long and tearful standing ovation. What happened next was a senior year filled with surprises.

In October, she was crowned homecoming queen with a lovely tiara atop her lovely, hairless head. The next day, her smiling face filled the front page of the Lansing State Journal, which carried her photo along with a cover story about her brave response to alopecia. In March, she sang and danced on stage in the high school musical *Anything Goes*. She wore a wig for the show because it made sense with the costume, but as soon as the performance was over, she took it off. She was accepted to Kalamazoo College and learned the tiny liberal arts school already has a female student with alopecia, who also eschews a wig in favor of her true appearance.

Caitlin's journey with alopecia forced her to take an unwelcome spiritual journey, but one she's glad she experienced. By realizing that her friends and schoolmates accepted her so completely, Caitlin finally learned to accept herself and the life God created for her.

— Marybeth Hicks

An author and speaker, Marybeth Hicks is the weekly syndicated family columnist for the Washington Times *newspaper in Washington, D.C. She is the author of* Bringing up Geeks: How to Protect Your Kid's Childhood in a Grow-Up-Too-Fast World *and* The Perfect World Inside My Minivan: One Mom's Journey Through the Streets of Suburbia, *selected by the Catholic Press Association as one of the three most outstanding family books for 2006. Marybeth and her husband, Jim, a law professor, live in the Midwest with their four children, Katie, eighteen; Betsy, sixteen; Jimmy, thirteen; and Amy, ten. Visit www.marybethhicks.com.*

Chapter 4

The Lighter Side of Surviving

The Incense That Burned My Pride Away

It was the week before Christmas when I got the call asking me if I would be able to serve at the altar for Christmas Mass. In my ten-year-old world, altar serving was nothing I took lightly. As one who has always enjoyed the spotlight, altar serving was my chance to bask in the bliss that accompanies playing a crucial role in the Mass. That year all of the carefully wrapped gifts under my tree paled in comparison to the anticipation of serving what in my mind was the "Super Bowl" of Masses.

Because I was to serve at the 8:00 a.m. Mass, my family woke in the wee hours of Christmas morning to exchange gifts. My favorite was a handsome blue denim jacket—just the kind I had been hoping for. I tried it on and admired myself in the mirror. "You can wear that to church today," my mom said, watching my beaming face.

As I did not want to even contemplate being late for the occasion, I had insisted that I be driven to the Cathedral of the Holy Spirit Parish a full hour before Mass. Shortly before 7:00 a.m., I proudly walked in to the sacristy and hung up my new jacket on the coat rack. I timidly looked at everyone's eyes to see if they had cast a glance at my new coat. The other server had not served nearly as many Masses as I had, so I informed him that I would make sure everything flowed smoothly. The priest took us both aside to inform us of the subtle differences that separated Christmas from a "regular" Mass.

"Now," Fr. Tom Richter said, "which one of you wants to carry the incense in during the procession?" I eagerly volunteered, reveling in the prospect of such a task. I listened confidently as he explained how the thurible should be held and the incense disposed of after the procession.

As was expected, the church was packed. Every pew was filled to capacity and folding chairs had been placed along the sides to contain the overflow. I processed into the church to the sound of "Joy to the World" and gave subtle nods to family and friends I saw along the way.

After bowing before the altar, I walked off into the sacristy to dispose of the incense. Surrounded by the sweet frankincense smoke, I tried to remember exactly what Fr. Richter had said about its disposal. I looked at the garbage can and the sink, but both places seemed like an unlikely place for such blessed material. As I contemplated the situation, I heard the "Let us pray" cue over the church's loudspeaker—my cue to bring up the big red book to the priest. I had told the other server that I would be doing that today and was not about to forfeit a job of such importance. I quickly opted for putting the old incense back into the incense box and hurried back into the church, only to find to my disappointment that the other server had already brought up the prayer book.

Mass progressed without incident until we neared the Eucharistic Prayer. Then, I noticed that through a crack in the sacristy door, which was located right next to the chairs of the altar servers, a steady, sweet-smelling smoke was escaping. Realizing this was most likely as a result of my manner of disposing the incense, I quickly left my post as altar server and hurried to investigate.

Smoke filled the entire room, burning my eyes as I walked toward the box of incense. The burning incense I had foolishly placed in with its unburned counterparts had ignited the entire

box. *Here it is, Christmas Mass, and I have set the church on fire!*
I thought. As I coughed through the thick smoke, I tried with
no success to open a locked window. I looked desperately for
something to extinguish the burning coals. Though there was
an abundance of white towels throughout the sacristy, they all
had a cross embroidered on them. After a moment of considering
using one of them, I became fairly certain that the road to hell
was paved with sinners who had desecrated holy cloths to put out
sacristy fires. I looked at the mini-fridge containing the unblessed
wine but was just as certain that the inner circles of hell held
sinners guilty of crimes no less severe than using wine for such a
purpose.

I looked briefly at my new denim jacket, realizing its potential,
but then quickly opted for using a box of tissues I saw. They worked
wonderfully but in the opposite way I had envisioned. Immediately,
they were set aflame compounding my already dire situation. Then,
though it pained me to do it, I took my denim jacket down from
the wall, scooped up the burning coals, and cast them down upon
the linoleum floor, stomping on my new jacket.

After I was certain that the flames were extinguished, I
quickly returned to my post at the altar smelling much holier than
before. As I stood by the altar, the priest covered his microphone,
asking me if everything was OK. I told him that there had been
a problem but I had taken care of everything. After a skeptical
smile, he resumed the Mass.

After receiving communion, I went back to the sacristy to
assess the damage. To my horror, I found that the coals had not
only burned through my jacket but were melting through the
linoleum floor, emitting the putrid smell of burning plastic.
I realized that I could not solve the situation on my own and
humbly went to get help.

The line for communion still stretched through the nave
of the church. I could not wait until it was finished. As Fr.
Richter was handing out the Eucharist, I walked up to him and

whispered, "I set the box of incense on fire, and now it's burning on the floor of the sacristy."

Father was quick to act. He halted Mass, and I followed him quickly. He filled a basin with water from a sink in the corner and poured it on the simmering incense coals. He gave me an understanding glance and said, "Well, I had better get back to Mass." I looked at the melted indents in the floor and my ruined Christmas present. Then my glance fell upon the sink in the corner. How could I not have noticed and thought to use it? The solution seemed as simple now as it had seemed difficult then.

After church that day, I threw my coat in the garbage outside the church. I realized several days later that my wallet containing a considerable amount of my Christmas money had been in the coat pocket.

In a manner of speaking, I went into that church that day prideful, richly dressed, and with a wallet full of a considerable amount of money for a ten-year-old boy. Somehow during the course of the Mass, through setting the church on fire, I had been forced to abandon my pride, give up my coat, and "donate" my money to the local dumpster.

Such things should perhaps be our reason for attending church in the first place. We come to Mass to learn humility. We go to church to learn to detach ourselves from the things of this world. We go to church to realize that happiness does not come through money and vanity. Many people are able to learn these three important lessons from listening to and reflecting on the Scriptures read during the Mass. For me, it took something a little more and a little hotter.

– Matt Fern

Matt Fern lives in Bozeman, Montana. He is a recent film studies graduate in and is currently pursuing a career in movie making.

G.P.S. S.O.S

"Our global positioning system contract just ran out."

Surviving Kid Country

I'm not sure why so many parenting experts write books. It seems like a waste of paper when there are dozens of field guides that provide valuable information on dealing with wild bears.

From my experience, you can substitute the word "child" for "bear" in any randomly selected book about camping and get the most effective tips about raising children.

For your convenience, I have provided the following summary, which includes everything you need to know to survive a week-long camping trip in Yosemite National Park—or to spend two hours with a child under the age of ten.

Humans and children can live in the same environment. While nothing can guarantee your safety in kid country, learning about children and their behavior can significantly reduce your risk of being mauled or, worse yet, driven crazy. Here are some basic tips:

- First, some basic facts about children. Children can climb trees. Children have an excellent sense of smell and better eyesight than most people think. Children will aggressively defend their food when threatened. Children often hide from people. But, just because you don't see a child, doesn't mean one isn't around. Remember, the most dangerous children often appear cute and friendly at first.

- Stay alert! Keep an eye out for signs of children. Look for claw or bite marks on trees, furniture, or siblings. Children also leave marks on walls, bathroom mirrors, and automobile upholstery. Tracks, trampled vegetation, or popsicle droppings are all clues that children may be nearby. Try not to surprise a child. If a child hears you coming, it will usually avoid you.

- Children have insatiable appetites and are attracted to junk food. They will tear apart a house while looking for salty or sweet snacks. Keep all Doritos, Twinkies, and HoHos in a secure food locker. Children will attempt to take food, even if you are holding it in your hand. And children remember easy sources of food. One taste of chocolate chip cookies and a child can be hooked for life. If you see a child, remain calm. The child may be passing through and will keep going if it doesn't find anything to eat.

- There are many gruesome tales of parents being attacked, mauled, swatted, or stomped by children. If you see a child at a distance and the child doesn't see you, turn around and leave the area. Do not attempt to interact with the child.

- If a child approaches or stands on his or her hind legs to get a better look at you—stop. The child may be curious and non-aggressive. Stand tall, wave your arms, and speak in a loud and low voice. Say words such as "bedtime" or "broccoli." These will repel most children. Back away slowly.

- If a child does attack, play dead. Curl up in a ball with your hands behind your neck. Lie still and quiet until the child wanders away.

That last tip is also effective when your wife wants you to clean the garage and you're watching a football game on television.

– Tim Bete

Tim Bete is author of the books In The Beginning ... There Were No Diapers *and* Guide to Pirate Parenting. *You can read more of his writing at www.TimBete.com.*

A Wheel Dilemma

"Now comes the hard part."

Survivors' Humor

What I Learned from Noah

Everything I need to know I learned from Noah's Ark...

1) Don't miss the boat.
2) Remember that we are all in the same boat.
3) Plan ahead. It wasn't raining when Noah built the Ark.
4) Stay fit. When you're sixty, someone may ask you to do something really big.
5) Don't listen to critics. Just get on with the job that needs to be done.

The End Is Near!

A local priest and a pastor were fishing on the side of the road. They thoughtfully made a sign saying, "The end is near! Turn yourself around now before it's too late!" and showed it to each passing car. One driver didn't appreciate the sign and shouted at them, "Leave us alone, you religious nuts!"

All of a sudden they heard a big splash. They looked at each other, and the priest said to the pastor, "You think maybe we should have just said 'Bridge out' instead?"

Father Murphy Walks into a Bar

Father Murphy walked into a bar and said to the first man he met, "Do you want to go to heaven?"

The man said, "I do, Father." The priest said, "Then stand over there against the wall."

Then the priest asked the second man, "Do you want to go to heaven?"

"Certainly, Father," was the man's reply. "Then stand over there against the wall," said the priest.

Then Father Murphy walked up to Paddy and said, "Do you want to go to heaven?" Paddy said, "No, I don't, Father." The priest said, "I don't believe this. You mean to tell me that when you die you don't want to go to heaven?"

Paddy said, "Oh, when I die, yes. I thought you were getting a group together to go right now."

Survivor: Suburbia

"Here we have reality TV, son. The set is in the shop."

Surviving *Survivor*

It's not too early to start your Halloween planning. I can tell it's time because stores are overflowing with candy and my kids are just finishing off their booty from last Halloween.

This year, our family is dressing up as reality TV stars. After all, there's nothing more frightening, and we've been practicing for our roles all year. We don't have satellite television or a deluxe cable package, but every day in our home is like a reality show.

If you think spending four weeks on a deserted island with a bunch of strangers (à la *Survivor*) is scary, try spending four minutes with my kids in the aisle of candy at the supermarket. You'll beg to be voted out of the store.

Here are some of the ghastly, real-life TV listings from my own experience.

Trading Spaces: The family prepares for child #4 by putting the girls into one bedroom. In the process, the source of that "unusual odor" is found under a bed.

The Simple Life: No one wants to go to the grocery store, so the family attempts to survive the weekend eating casseroles made from Ritz Crackers, olives, and peanut butter.

The Amazing Race: Dad uses NASCAR-style driving skills in a futile attempt to get the kids to school on time.

Big Brother: The boy torments his younger sister by hiding her juice cup. Later, she gets even by biting him on the leg.

Big Sister: The boy searches for earplugs as his older sister attempts to enter the *Guinness Book of World Records* with a six-hour whining fit about parents who are unfair.

Extreme Combover: Dad continues to lose his hair at an alarming rate but thinks he's found a solution.

American Idle: The kids say they're "bored" and have "nothing to play with." Dad entertains them by filling two trash cans with toys.

Last Sibling Standing: Similar to *Sibling Boxing*. First one to cry loses.

Who Wants to Empty the Trash? Family members avoid emptying the trash for as long as possible. Contestants each receive one lifeline telephone call from a friend who tries to provide an alibi to get the contestant out of the house.

Name That Sound! This new show (which was originally called *Who Put the Golf Ball in the Garbage Disposal?*) was invented by a child who is also on the show *America's Most Wanted*.

Trading Louses: A lice outbreak at school forces mom and dad to purchase a nit comb.

Temptation Freezer: Temptation Freezer is an unscripted dramatic series in which a family's freezer is filled with gourmet ice cream to test and explore the strength of their willpower. Will the ice cream last the night? Dad can hear the Cookies & Cream calling his name.

Fear Factor: Last week the babysitter canceled and Mom and Dad had to spend an entire night with the kids. This week, the two-year-old has polished off a pint of blueberries, two containers of prune yogurt, and a box of raisins. Mom and Dad debate who will change the next diaper.

Viewer discretion is advised.

– Tim Bete

Tim Bete's biography appears after "Surviving Kid Country" earlier in this chapter.

Bounced by Bureaucracy

"No receipt, no return."

The Scales of Injustice

No denying it. Can't get out of it. What is, is ...

Nope. No amount of common sense was going to make me step on that horrible, annoying, lying doctor's scale! Just a few days earlier, a friend who works at my doctor's clinic had told me that a new policy had been adopted respecting a patient's right to refuse getting weighed.

"*Rceually?*" I asked enthusiastically, but not quite believing it could be true. I had put off more doctor appointments than I could count on both hands and feet because of that accursed scale. So without hesitation, I foolishly swallowed the "I-don't-have-to-get-weighed" concept quicker than a Reese's cup and, within days, found myself getting my blood pressure taken while I stared at the metal monster.

I answered politely as the petite nurse made small talk, but in truth, I was still having a hard time believing that I wouldn't have to take off my coat, shoes, rings, and necklace before stepping onto the scale of humility. (They always add five pounds, you know.) *Good thing I got my hair cut, cleaned out my belly button, and cut my toenails—just in case.* I inwardly chuckled.

The tiny nurse took my temperature. She seemed nice. So far, so good. I began to relax. For the next few moments, I talked about my sore throat and things were just peachy—until she chirped the ghastly words, "Okaaayyy now, let's just hop onto the scale and get a quick weight." How could something that was uttered in such a syrupy sweet voice make me so uneasy?

My pulse increased slightly, but I remained calm. *It's my decision,* I thought. *I'm a mother of three children. I can make my own decisions.* So, in my most grown-up, confident-woman voice, I said politely, "I don't care to get weighed today, thank you." Inwardly, I smiled, triumphantly. *Wow, this is great! I am in charge!* I felt empowered!

Ms. Petite Nurse smiled and answered in a singsong voice,

"Oh, but I would *really* like to get your weight today. You haven't been here in a while."

Pulse increase. "Uh, I'm just here for a sore throat and to ask a few questions. I'll get weighed another time." Fib.

Ms. Small Fry smiled angelically, "You don't have to *look* if you don't want to."

Annoyance quickly overshadowed my growing panic, so I gave her a strained smiled and said, "I *know* that. I don't *care* to be weighed today." I then crossed my legs and looked the other direction. *Geesh, she needs to get a life. I'm not pregnant, and I don't have high blood pressure.*

Suddenly, my excuses seemed a little weak, and the better part of me began to feel some compassion for this tiny nurse who was only trying to do her job. I was just about to give in and "step up to the plate," so to speak, when Nurse Wretched angrily barked, "Come on, now … Just let me get your weight … It's really no big deal!"

NO BIG DEAL??? Is this woman daft? I suddenly wanted to stand up straight—all 5'8" of me—and say, "Don't you know that I could squash you if I sat on you?" *How much could this twerp weigh—eighty-five pounds, dripping wet?*

Sticking up for myself had never been one of my strong points—I had always been taught to be polite, respectful, and kind. Unfortunately, my experience was that many people view those attributes as a "welcome mat" that says, "Go ahead, walk all over me."

Ms. Dainty Dictator boldly opened her mouth and began to ask again, when suddenly I found determination I didn't know I possessed. I stared at her with a look that said, "One of us is going to win … and it's *NOT* going to be you." (There goes my "Nice Lady of the Year" award.)

Ms. Size Zero then clamped her mouth shut, grabbed her clipboard, and furiously scribbled the word, "REFUSED."

How rude! I thought. I would have much preferred the word,

"Declined." Nevertheless, I smiled victoriously as I followed her from the room.

– Elizabeth Schmeidler

Elizabeth Schmeidler is happily married and mother to three wonderful sons. Also a singer-songwriter, Elizabeth has composed and recorded three CDs of inspirational music. Her music can be heard on many radio and Internet stations and ordered through CDbaby.com. As an author of novels, short stories, children's stories, and poetry, she continues to write and sing in her pursuit to do God's will. She can be contacted at cdmusic@eaglecom.net.

Survivors' One-Liners

- Don't let your worries get the best of you. Remember, Moses started out as a basket case.

- Many folks want to serve God, but only as advisors.

- It is easier to preach ten sermons than it is to live one.

- When you get to your wit's end, you'll find God lives there.

- Quit griping about your church; if it was perfect, you couldn't belong.

- If the church wants a better priest, it only needs to pray for the one it has.

- God Himself does not propose to judge a man until he is dead. So why should you?

- Peace starts with a smile.

- We were called to be witnesses, not lawyers or judges.

- Be ye fishers of men. You catch them; God will clean them.

- Coincidence is when God chooses to remain anonymous.

- God doesn't call the qualified; He qualifies the called.

- God promises a safe landing, not a calm passage.

- He who angers you, controls you!

- If God is your copilot, swap seats!

- Prayer: Don't give God instructions; just report for duty!

- The task ahead of us is never as great as the Power behind us.

- The will of God will never take you to where the grace of God will not protect you.

- We don't change the message; the message changes us.

- You can tell how big a person is by what it takes to discourage him.

Chapter 5

His Healing Touch

Never Say Never

Paul Walsh was seventeen years old when the car he was driving hit a tree on Chester Pike in suburban Philadelphia on an icy December night in 1983. One doctor described his head injuries as the equivalent of dropping an egg on a cement sidewalk. Not only was his skull shattered, but every bone in his face was broken, and there was a tear in his brain. Doctors at Crozier Chester Medical Center said he was irreversibly brain damaged and would never regain consciousness. But as the old saying goes, "Never say never."

On Saturday, May 14, 2005, Paul Walsh received a bachelor's degree in liberal arts from Neumann College in Aston, Pennsylvania. "I'd like to teach special ed," said the thirty-eight-year-old graduate, who is employed as a full-time health care associate with Elwyn, Inc., a residential day program for the mentally disadvantaged. "I'd like to continue working with mentally disadvantaged persons."

Paul's recovery from massive head injuries in 1983 was "unexplained, on a purely medical and scientific basis," said one of the physicians who treated him, Dr. Michael Ryan. In a written statement, Dr. Ryan said, "It is my feeling that without the help of the supernatural influence, Paul would today be dead or continue to be in a comatose state."

Although he recalls little of his four month ordeal following the accident, his mother, Betty Walsh, remembers every detail, from the moment she got the phone call on the night of the accident. "The nurse told me to come to the hospital right away," said the mother of ten from Ridley Park, Pennsylvania. "It was hard to even recognize Paul. His face was so swollen, like a pumpkin, and totally wrapped in bandages. It didn't look very good, but I could tell that he recognized my voice because he moved when he heard me."

After ten hours of surgery the following day, during which Paul lost four-and-half times the amount of blood in his body, he was transferred to Crozier Chester Medical Center, where his condition remained critical.

At first, he seemed to be improving and was even talking a little, but there was a suspicious fluid dripping out of his nose. Everyone thought he had a cold, and a month went by before doctors discovered that the fluid wasn't from nasal congestion—it was spinal fluid. A CT scan revealed a tear in Paul's brain.

"That's when they realized he was worse off than they had thought," Betty said.

Doctors tried to repair the tear, but the inside of Paul's head was too shattered. They resorted to draining the fluid with spinal taps and then a catheter, but Paul's condition continued to deteriorate. He began slipping in and out of consciousness.

Another CT scan revealed that he had hydrocephalus, and the ventricles of his brain were filling with fluid. Doctors prepared him for emergency surgery to put a shunt in his head to drain the fluid. However, they discovered yet another serious complication: he had also developed spinal meningitis. "At that point, there was no hope," Betty said. "The ventricles just kept filling with fluid, and this flattened the frontal lobe of his brain, which one doctor told me would affect his whole personality."

Even though Paul was technically alive, in essence, he was gone. "They kept saying, 'You have to stop hoping. The way he is now is the way he's going to be. He is permanently and irreversibly brain damaged.'" But Betty was not about to give up on her son. Even though she had nine other children at home, she felt like the woman in the Bible who had ten coins but lost one and could not stop searching until she found it.

"We just decided Paul needed a miracle," Betty said. "In the end, if Paul didn't get better, I would accept it, but in the meantime, I was really going to believe I could have a miracle, and I would at least pray with faith."

A woman from St. Madeline's in Ridley Park gave her five prayer cards for people who were in the process of beatification and needed a miracle. Every day after Mass, she and her mother would go to the hospital and pray the Rosary over Paul, then say the five prayers. "Whenever I came to the Padre Pio prayer, Paul blessed himself, even though he was totally unconscious," Betty said.

Several people witnessed the phenomenon, including a few nurses. Betty decided to call a local group of Padre Pio devotees and report what was happening. They decided to send someone to the hospital with one of the gloves worn by Padre Pio over the bloody stigmata wounds in his hands. On Monday, March 12, Paul was blessed with the relic, and within days, one of his many serious ailments had miraculously vanished.

Betty called the group again, and on April 6, 1984, the glove was once again brought to Paul and laid on his head. "I knew immediately something happened because it was like an electric shock went through him," Betty said. "He opened his eyes and looked around the room, very clear-eyed. Then he fell back into the coma again, but I just knew something had happened."

She was right. The next day, when she returned to the hospital, she was shocked to find her son sitting in a chair and watching television. He turned and said, "Hi, Mom."

The nurse rushed in and said, "He's been talking all day!" When the nurse called the neurosurgeon to tell him Paul was talking, the doctor said, "That's impossible!" and hung up on her.

But it was true. "They gave Paul another CT scan, and all the doctor kept saying was, 'I don't believe this. I don't believe this.' The frontal lobe of his brain wasn't smashed anymore."

An even more inexplicable event happened a few days later, on Easter Sunday morning, when Paul and his roommate woke up to find a man standing at the foot of Paul's bed. Described as "an old priest in a brown robe," Paul thought it was Betty's brother, Charley, who bears a remarkable resemblance to Padre Pio.

"I remember being very certain that my Uncle Charley had been in to visit me," Paul said. "I did see him. He was very happy and smiled at me. And then he left the room."

Betty knew it couldn't have been Charley because he lives in Boston. She folded up a picture of Padre Pio, hiding the name, and showed it to Paul. "That's who visited me," he said. "Isn't that Uncle Charley?"

Weeks later, Paul Walsh walked out of Crozier Chester Medical Center, completely healed.

If there was any doubt in their minds that Padre Pio had interceded in Paul's healing, those doubts were put to rest a year after the accident when the family received an unexpected phone call from Bill Rose, who lived on the property where Paul hit the tree. Rose claimed he heard the crash the night of the accident and ran outside to find Paul lying on the ground with his face in a gutter. He knew that Paul was dying, and while someone called for an ambulance, he held Paul's head up out of the gutter and prayed for his soul.

"Within three to five minutes of your son's accident," he told Betty, "I dedicated him to Padre Pio."

To this day, Paul admits he still wonders "why me?" But that doesn't stop him from telling his story whenever he can. "I'm not doing this for myself," Paul said. "I want to give other people hope."

– Susan Brinkmann

Susan Brinkmann, O.C.D.S., is a correspondent for the Catholic Standard & Times *of Philadelphia and member of the Third Order of Discalced Carmelites. Formerly a historical fiction writer with two novels published by HarperCollins, Susan has devoted her life and talents to building up the Church and tearing down the culture of death. She currently serves as a staff writer for Living His Life Abundantly International – www.lhla.org.*

Battling with Pregnancy

My first pregnancy was unplanned and, in turn, brought tremendous unplanned joy to my husband and me. All was well, as we eagerly anticipated the birth of our precious child. But then I was diagnosed with a rare, seriously debilitating pregnancy-related illness called hyperemesis gravidarum. Its cause is unknown, but it is akin to being violently allergic to one's own baby.

By four months into the pregnancy, I had lost fourteen percent of my total body weight. I couldn't eat or drink. I had liver dysfunction and jaundice, and I began to hallucinate from starvation, dehydration, and inadequate medical care. I couldn't work, walk, talk, eat, drink, read, watch TV, sit up, or do anything but lie still. Otherwise, I would vomit. There were no nausea-free periods. The vomiting was excessive, and life was a living nightmare.

My physicians were not adequately hydrating me, nor were they providing me with appropriate nutrition. These things were available and necessary in my case, but I was naïve. I didn't know I could be tube fed or receive continuous fluids at home. I simply wasn't told. Once my physicians learned that our child was unplanned, they totally disregarded our desire for our baby and treated my physical disease as though it were a psychosomatic disorder. They believed my illness meant my child was unwanted.

My husband couldn't help me. He didn't know what to do and thought I was either going to die or sustain permanent damage and mental morbidity. Everyone was telling us how abnormal my condition was, except the doctors, who weren't telling us anything.

After long suffering, neglect, and downright demoralization, I woke up one morning and just snapped. I felt I could not go on even one more day in that condition. I believed abortion was the only way out, made the appointment, and went through the sickening, heartbreaking, permanent experience of abortion.

When it was over, my husband and I were horrified and hurt by what we had done, tormented by the deep, soul-shaking loss of our child. Yet I had not been pro-life. I had been raised by educated liberals to be "pro-choice." I accepted this belief without question and thought anyone who didn't was barbaric. I also bought into the media hype that portrayed abortion opponents as violent, uneducated, and hypocritical religious fanatics. The church I attended supported abortion. I couldn't find a reason to oppose it, but I admit I never really looked for one.

But after my abortion, something electric and wonderful was absent from my body and our lives. Only the loss of a child could cause this kind of despair, and we realized that if he or she was a person, *all* unborn babies are. Of course, our wanting our child was not what made him or her a person. And as per our Constitution, people have certain inalienable rights; among them is life. We came to understand that abortion is the ultimate violation of civil rights. And the intriguing thing is that abortion itself obliterated any support we had for abortion. We learned the hard way.

Eleven years have passed. As my child's due date approaches, remembering remains difficult. Every day there is love and longing but unspeakable pain. However, I am helped by helping others. With God's support, guidance, and abundant provision, I wrote the very first comprehensive help and information book on hyperemesis gravidarum. God has used this book to touch and save hearts and lives, and I am privileged to have been used by Him. I am comforted by this and God's promise of mercy. Also, time has passed, and I have had other children who have proved to be a beautiful and wonderful distraction.

While my second child died in a miscarriage, my third pregnancy was much like the first. But the medical difficulties of my fourth pregnancy were a torture I could never have fathomed.

It seemed I could not possibly survive. I vomited over forty times a day at my worst, couldn't eat or drink for seventy-seven days, and was on continuous IVs and tube feedings at home. I spent over a month in the hospital and had multiple X-rays and more than twelve medications, beginning in the fifth week of pregnancy. I developed a potentially life-threatening staph infection and was completely bedridden for greater than thirty unbelievably long weeks. I wanted a way out, an easier way than suffering through it all. But ultimately, I knew that my own death was preferable to killing another child in an abortion.

The primary reason I was able to persevere was God. I pressed on because of my faith in Christ and His promise to walk with me. I trusted Him enough to give Him my health, my comfort, even my life should He require it. Christ forgave the adulterous woman, but He also told her to go and *sin no more*. I knew that I could not expect Christ to take my grief and repentance seriously if I turned around and aborted again. I was finally able to focus on the fact that He gave me His all, so I decided to give Him mine.

I survived and will continue to do so with Christ. I am raising two beautiful children who are certainly God's huge blessing. My book, *Beyond Morning Sickness: Battling Hyperemesis Gravidarum*, not only continues to help others avoid the devastation that our family experienced through abortion, but it also reaches out to those who, sadly, have not. I have learned to be grateful for my horrific pregnancy experiences because God used them to enable me to serve others in a meaningful way for Him. I have been in the delivery room with mothers and observed the birth of children who had previously been scheduled for termination. What a blessing it has been to witness those babies being born. I have watched their mothers cry tears of joy upon seeing them for the first time. Indeed, these are the only tears a mother should cry.

– Ashli McCall

Ashli McCall is a stay-at-home, homeschooling mother from Florida. Her book, Beyond Morning Sickness: Battling Hyperemesis Gravidarum, *as well as disease information and forums, can be found at www.beyondmorningsickness. com. Other excellent sources of support are hyperemesis.org and hghelp.com.*

A Doctor *and* a Catholic

There never was a time in my medical career when "the birth control question" did not hang over my head. As a cradle Catholic, I took for granted that the Church's teachings on contraception must be followed in my own life. But I often wondered how my Catholic faith should impact my medical practice. Was it okay to give "the pill" to other women, as long as I did not use it myself? The answers did not come easily.

When I first started college at Creighton University, becoming a doctor was not even on the radar. *That's too ambitious for me,* I determined. My boyfriend, Art, and I expected that we would be married within a few years. Since we both wanted a family, I felt I could not afford the time for medical school. However, by the end of our freshman year, we went our separate ways. My options suddenly seemed wide open. I could not stop thinking about applying to medical school. So I took one tentative step at a time, and by my senior year, I was accepted to Creighton University School of Medicine.

But the thrill of attaining my goal was tempered with a growing dilemma. I was training to be a family practice doctor, but I was also a Catholic. I had specifically chosen Creighton, a Catholic Jesuit university, to protect my faith during a time when young people often drifted away. I knew in my heart that my Catholic faith was the true way to Christ. Still, there seemed to be an unwritten rule that a doctor must leave her ethical beliefs outside the patient's exam room. Even though I knew that contraception violated the natural law and God's plan for marriage, was it really relevant to how I would practice medicine?

After my second year in medical school, Art came back into my life, and the embers of our earlier romance reignited. Within a matter of weeks, we became engaged, and a year and a half later, on December 29, 2000, we married. Art had shared my commitment to wait until after marriage before becoming sexually intimate. We also agreed to learn and use Natural Family Planning. I was doing everything that I thought a "good" Catholic should do.

Shortly before I graduated from medical school, I decided to dig a little deeper into my birth control dilemma. I took on a research project regarding whether it was morally acceptable for a Catholic physician to prescribe contraception. I had hoped to confirm the mainstream thought that my personal beliefs did not have to carry over into patient care. Yet the more I learned about contraception, the more concerned I was about the potential side effects. While most are minor, some are serious, such as the risk of stroke and heart attack. There is also a possible link to breast cancer. Fertility is not a disease, so why would we use such powerful chemicals to suppress a natural bodily function? Doesn't the Hippocratic oath say, "First do no harm"?

Even now, most women still do not understand how the pill works. Most of the time, it blocks ovulation, so no egg is released. But there are times when ovulation does occur. In those instances, the pill changes the lining of the uterus so that a fertilized embryo cannot implant. This is an abortion. I knew I could never perform an abortion, but was this really any different?

Beyond the medical arguments, I found that contraception sends the wrong message about sex and even encourages women to be treated as objects.

"What does the language of sex say? In its natural form it says: 'I find you attractive. I trust you with my most intimate self. I would never hurt you. I desire to be with you completely and absolutely, even to have a child with you.' By contrast, contraception sex says: 'I desire to be one with you, but not fully. I want to engage in an act of great but momentary pleasure with you, but I am unwilling to accept responsibility for anything that may follow; I do not want my life that tightly bound up with yours." (Flannery, K: Koterski, J. "Paul VI was Right." *America* 169: 7-11, 1993.)

These were strong arguments, but I still was not sure they applied to my medical practice. Then I found another argument. The classic moral definition of a scandal is to cooperate with another in an evil action. If contraception is evil, it stood to reason that a physician who supplies oral contraceptives is participating in her own form of scandal. Jesus said, "It would be better for anyone who leads astray one of these little ones who believes in me to be drowned by a millstone around his neck in the depths of the sea. What terrible things will come upon the world by scandal! "Woe to that man through whom scandal comes" (Mt 18:6-7). That passage came through loud and clear. In fact, it haunted me over the coming years.

But the battle wasn't over. I reasoned that I was not corrupting these women; they had already come into my office with their own viewpoint. Besides, I wanted to be liked by my patients and fit in with my colleagues. If I did not give patients the birth control they asked for, I would be viewed as some kind of religious radical. To be honest, I just was not strong enough to do that.

So I graduated from medical school and began my family medicine residency in Sioux City, Iowa. The issue was not resolved, but I just kept praying. "I'm going to *try* not to prescribe the pill," I told myself. I was not convincing anyone. The first time my values were challenged was a few months into residency. A petite, sixteen-year-old blonde came in to discuss birth control. I took a deep breath and tried to give her the kind of talk you see in the movies where everything changes after an impassioned speech that evokes tears and opens minds. "You are better than that," I firmly told her. I talked to her about abstinence and how precious her body was. But instead of a light turning on, she only stared at me blankly and said she would still like the pill.

Biting back tears of failure, I hurried down the hall to another doctor and had him prescribe the birth control my patient wanted. I had clung to my values, but it felt like such a mockery. Instead of giving this girl a prescription in my own handwriting, she now clutched one written by the hand of a doctor down the hall. In the end, it was all the same, wasn't it?

A few months later, I assisted at a C-section in which the woman was getting a tubal ligation. When the surgeon asked me to hold the clamp as he cut the fallopian tube, I stepped back and had someone else do the deed. Again, it felt like a mockery. In the end, the sterilization would be performed with or without me. Why was I risking my professional reputation and making myself out to be a weirdo when the patient outcome was going to be the same either way? Some doctors reasoned with me that birth control was the lesser of two evils: better to use birth control than to be sixteen and pregnant. (By the way, the sixteen-year-old blonde who had left with contraceptives was back in the clinic the following year for pregnancy care.)

I was tired of the stress. I decided that my faith is between me and God and that my patients' beliefs are not my business. End of story ... or not.

I completed my residency in 2004 and took a job in rural North Dakota. In the weeks before I started work, the issue of birth control continued to nag at me. I prayed to God and often talked to myself, promising that I would tell the business manager that I did not want to prescribe birth control. Whenever I was face-to-face with him, however, I chickened out. So several times a week, when a patient came and asked for birth control, I swallowed hard and quickly wrote out the prescription. But it was not an issue I could smother. My Catholic faith is such a huge part of my identity, it kept nagging at me. One Sunday, I considered becoming an extraordinary minister of the Eucharist at church, but something held me back. Extraordinary ministers needed to be Catholics in good standing. Was that me? Was I betraying God by helping people go against His natural law? Deep down, I was not at all sure I was in good standing, but as long as no one noticed, I could continue in my denial. I did not volunteer in order to avoid the question.

I was playing hide and seek with God. Art listened to my feelings and told me he was ready to support me, no matter which path I took. By now, we had two small children, Ben and Maya. I often wondered how I would explain to them someday that we did not believe birth control was right but I still gave it out almost daily. Yet, a doctor cannot survive if she does not follow the mainstream. How could I survive as a family practitioner and still follow God without compromise? *God, if you want me to do this, you have to make me stronger,* I prayed.

After three years in practice, it seemed my prayers were answered. I accepted a position in Bismarck as a primary care physician affiliated with St. Alexius, the area's Catholic hospital. It was a perfect opportunity to make a break with my contraceptive practices.

I began my new practice, finally ready to stand by my values. *This is a Catholic facility,* I reasoned. *It should be simple to avoid birth control.* It is never that clear-cut, though. God had given me a supportive environment, but the final step was up to me. Soon, a patient came in for birth control. *OK, God,* I thought, *Let's do this.*

"I'm sorry," I said, "I don't prescribe birth control." I forced the words out of my mouth in a voice that sounded firmer than I felt. The patient accepted that, and decided she wanted to complete her exam anyway. I told her she would need to find another physician to get the prescription. After she left the examining room, I heard from her mother, who was a friend of mine.

"Where is she supposed to go?" the mother asked. "She does not know anyone else." She was not angry—it was an honest question. I caved in and wrote the prescription. But this time was different. I felt horrible. I had moved to a new community for a new job and had been determined to start fresh, without compromise. But at the first challenge, I had failed.

I do not know if I was looking for a sign, or advice, or what, but I got onto the Internet. I landed on the Catholic Medical

Association website. There, I stumbled on a familiar name. Dr. John Breheny was an ethicist I had met during my residency in Sioux City. We attended the same church, and I had great respect for him. Thanking the Holy Spirit for this "coincidence," I quickly sent him an e-mail about my moral dilemma. Dr. Breheny responded right away, making some very strong arguments:

"You know that the Church teaches that contraception is wrong ... In fact, it is harmful to women (physically, emotionally, relationally, and spiritually), and harmful for men, families and society as well. If something is seriously wrong, then *it is wrong to participate in it or facilitate the action.* Think, for a moment, if you lived in Oregon where assisted suicide is legal. Now, most physicians are still against this. Would it be the same decision to write a prescription for a lethal dose of narcotics (a) because this is what the patient asked for; (b) it is legal; (c) other physicians are doing it; and/or (d) if you didn't do it, someone else would? In any case, if something is wrong, then it is wrong to participate in it. If something is wrong, and harmful to women, then it is not a good way to practice medicine. In fact, it is possible to survive and thrive without prescribing [contraception]. I hope you can come to see that. I'm not making it up. Again, I have met physicians who have gone down this same path, and more continue to come along.

"In short, I am arguing that not prescribing is not only the right thing to do, it is a good thing for your patients. Having said that, I know this is not an easy decision. It clearly is easier to stay with the status quo. Going against the current is always hard, and our modern American culture has a lot invested in medical control of women's fertility. It isn't just the personal and social values, the medical "standards of care," etc.; there is a lot of money invested as well. But I am convinced that it is important and necessary if we are to transform our culture with the Gospel and necessary to serve women's health effectively."

As I read his words, tears filled my eyes. Each line was filled with the arguments I had hidden from for so long. I felt liberated. I can only describe it as the power of the Holy Spirit. I had finally found the strength I needed. Within a week, I went from saying: "I do not *want* to do this" to clearly stating: "I am *not* doing this." The more I said it, the stronger I felt. Now, after a year in my new practice, my resolve is firm. My practice is growing, and I love going to work every day. I've finally learned that I can be a good doctor *and* a Catholic.

One unexpected surprise is that God is using my practice to support and assist families who use Natural Family Planning. Many have never seen a doctor who even understands how NFP works. There is such a wealth of medical information hidden in the charting used, and now I am learning how to tap into that resource. My next step is to return to Omaha to become a Medical Consultant for Creighton Model Natural Family Planning through the Pope Paul VI Institute. I have finally found a way to use my medical skills as a ministry, and I know that is where God wants me to be.

– Laura Archuleta

Laura Archuleta is a North Dakota native. She is married with two beautiful children and enjoys gardening, family time, and laughing. She practices family medicine in Mandan and Bismarck.

The Gift of Cancer

Several years ago, God gave Richard J. Cusack, Sr., the greatest possible gift. "It was cancer and the fear of dying," said the sixty-seven-year-old Cusack. "Through that gift He woke me up and showed me what life is all about and how wonderful it can be when you begin your journey closer to Him."

By anyone's estimation, Cusack was living the ideal life. A successful president of a benefits consulting firm in Wayne, Pennsylvania, he felt like he was standing on the top of the world on New Year's Eve, 1992. "I was at a party in a big home in Newtown Square, a hundred people, lots of champagne," Cusack said. "I had just turned fifty-two. When it came time for the toast, I remember turning to my wife, Martha, and saying, 'Well, I can finally say it. This is our time. We're on top of the world. We have the home, the shore place, the boat. We can travel. Our kids are grown. I'm just about ready to semi-retire.'"

Two months later, during a routine physical, a doctor found a lump in this throat. He was diagnosed with thyroid cancer. In an attempt to prolong his life, doctors performed a complete thyroidectomy, which meant removing the control mechanism for twenty-five different body functions, from hormones to sleep cycles.

"I couldn't eat anything. There was confusion, shaking, nervousness, memory problems. I was losing weight and looked emaciated. I began suffering from debilitating depression." In a matter of months, he said, "I went from the top of the world to the depths of hell."

Although he had faith to turn to God for help, it wasn't enough to sustain him through such an ordeal, even through he always went to Sunday Mass and thought he was a good Catholic. "But my business was the number one priority in my life. God was somewhere down the list."

Now that his time seemed short, and his suffering was so

excruciating, he began praying, but not for a miracle. He prayed to die. Every night before he went to bed, he would pray before a large portrait of the Blessed Mother, putting his hand on her face and begging her to ask God to take him from this world. "I never asked for a miracle because I never thought I deserved one," he said. "What did I ever do for God? People would say all the time that they understood how frightened I was about the cancer and I'd say, 'I'm not frightened about the cancer. I'm frightened about the final judgment.'"

Instead of answering his prayer for death, however, God chose a road that would lead to a whole new life. God's plan began to unfold the day Cusack's daughter introduced him to a nun who suggested he attend exposition of the Blessed Sacrament in their convent from 3:30 to 5:00 every day. At first he declined because of depression, but a few days later he changed his mind. He went and found comfort sitting in the presence of God.

One day, a tiny, eighty-year-old nun named Sister Theresa approached him after seeing him crying in the chapel so often. She took him by the hand and said, "Richard, you must have great faith and trust in God. You must work yourself closer to Him. No matter what the future holds, you need to begin a journey that will bring you closer to Him."

He decided to take her advice. First, he would replace laziness with sacrifice and change his life regardless of how much was left. He began to go to confession frequently, to attend daily Mass, and to visit the Blessed Sacrament.

Two years later, in 1994, he was still alive and gaining weight, even though he still had serious health problems. "I would continue to go before the Blessed Sacrament to thank Him for giving me each new day. However, I still believed my remaining time on earth was short, so I decided to really say 'yes' to Him for whatever time I had left."

That's when things began to happen. One of the sisters encouraged him to write down his experiences for others. He composed ten different brochures, which were widely distributed. He told his story on a Catholic radio show, *My Jesus Mercy,* and had so many callers he ended up with his own show, *For Those Who Hurt,* which ran for several years. He spoke wherever he was invited.

One Friday afternoon at 3:00 p.m., he was sitting in a perpetual adoration chapel, thanking God for all the extra time he had been given. "Before I arrive at my final judgment, is there something I can do for you here on earth?" he asked God. "What would be pleasing to you?"

He suddenly had an inspiration about making a beautiful holy card with a monstrance on the front and the words, "Do you really love me? Then come to me. Visit me before the Blessed Sacrament."

He went home and sketched out the card, including the message on the back, and took it to a printer. The initial printing was a hundred cards. He began giving them out, and was soon receiving requests for more cards.

He saw God's hand when he got a letter from Sister Roberta Ochs, president of the World Apostolate of Fatima in Portugal, saying that she had received a card and wanted 10,000 more to distribute to pilgrims. This was followed by another call from the Sisters of the Precious Blood in Manchester, New Hampshire, requesting 5,000 cards. Before long, the cards were circling the globe, and requests were coming in from everywhere. Accepting no donations, Cusack and his wife Martha box and ship thousands of cards every month from their home. They have distributed more than three million of them. Cusack returns every call personally. Any donations are given to the Sisters of the Precious Blood, who send the money to help seminarians studying for overseas missions.

"I can say there is a wonderful movement going on in the Catholic Church all over the world," he said. "Churches are opening up for adoration. People are bringing their fears and anxieties to Jesus."

That's the real story, he says. "Was what happened to me a miracle? The miracle isn't medical. I think the miracle is what the Holy Spirit has done with all this."

— Susan Brinkmann

Susan Brinkmann's biography appears after the story "Never Say Never" at the beginning of this chapter.

To order cards for distribution, write to For Those Who Hurt, 175 Strafford Ave., Building Four, Suite One, Wayne, PA 19087 or call 610-687-7660.

Against All Odds

I never considered myself unique, but people are constantly telling me that I am a miracle. To me, I was just an "ordinary" guy with realistic goals and big dreams. I was a nineteen-year-old student at the University of Texas and well on my way toward fulfilling my dream of one day becoming an orthopedic surgeon. On the night of February 17, 1981, I was studying for an organic chemistry test at the library with Sharon, my girlfriend of three years. Sharon had asked me to drive her back to her dormitory, as it was getting quite late. We got into my car, not realizing that just getting into a car would never quite be the same for me again.

I quickly noticed that my gas gauge was registering empty, so I pulled into a nearby convenience store to buy two dollars' worth of gas. "I'll be back in two minutes," I yelled to Sharon as I closed the door. But instead, those two minutes changed my life forever.

Entering the convenience store was like entering the twilight zone. On the outside I was a healthy, athletic, pre-med student, but on the inside I was just another statistic of a violent crime. I thought I was entering an empty store, but suddenly I realized it was not empty at all. Three individuals were in the process of committing a robbery, and my entrance into the store caught them by surprise. One of the them immediately shoved a .38 caliber handgun to my head, ordered me to the cooler, pushed me down on the floor, and pumped a bullet into the back of my head, execution-style. He obviously thought I was dead because he did not shoot me again. The trio of thieves finished robbing the store and left calmly.

Meanwhile, Sharon wondered why I had not returned. After seeing the three men leave the store, she really began to worry, as I was the last person she saw entering the store. She quickly went inside to look for me, but saw no one—only a nearly empty cash register containing one check and several pennies. Quickly, she ran down each aisle, shouting, "Mike, Mike."

Just then, the attendant appeared from the back of the store, shouting, "Lady, get down on the floor. I've just been robbed and shot at!"

Sharon quickly dropped to the floor, screaming, "Have you seen my boyfriend ... auburn hair?" The man did not reply but went back to the cooler, where he found me choking on my vomit. The attendant quickly cleaned my mouth and then called for the police and an ambulance.

Sharon was in shock. She was beginning to understand that I was hurt, but she could not begin to comprehend or imagine the severity of my injury.

When the police arrived, they immediately called the homicide division, as they did not think I would survive. The paramedic reported that she had never seen a person survive after being so severely wounded. At 1:30 a.m., my parents, who lived in Houston, were awakened by a telephone call from Brackenridge Hospital, advising them to come to Austin as soon as possible for they feared I would not make it through the night.

I did make it through the night, and early in the morning, the neurosurgeon decided to operate. He quickly informed my family and Sharon, however, that my chances of surviving the surgery were only 40/60. If this were not bad enough, the neurosurgeon further shocked my family by telling them what life would be like for me if I beat the odds and survived. He said I probably would never walk, talk, or be able to understand even simple commands.

My family was hoping and praying to hear even the slightest bit of encouragement from that doctor. Instead, his pessimistic words gave my family no reason to believe that I would be a functioning member of society ever again. But, once again, I beat the odds and survived the three-and-a-half hours of surgery.

Even though my family breathed a huge sigh of relief that I was still alive, the doctor cautioned that it still would be several days before I would be out of danger. With each passing day, however, I became stronger and stronger, and two weeks later I was well enough to be moved from the ICU to a private room. Granted, I still could not talk, my entire right side was paralyzed, and many people thought I could not understand, but at least I was stable. After one week in a private room, the doctors felt I had improved enough to be transferred by jet ambulance to Del Oro Rehabilitation Hospital in Houston.

My hallucinations—coupled with my physical problems—made my prognosis very bleak. As time passed, however, my mind began to clear, and, approximately six weeks later, my right leg began to move ever so slightly. Within seven weeks, my right arm slowly began to move, and at eight weeks, I uttered my first few words. My speech was extremely difficult and slow in the beginning, but at least it was a beginning.

I was starting to look forward to each new day to see how far I would progress. But just as I thought my life was finally looking brighter, I was tested by the hospital neuropsychologist. She explained to me that—judging by my test results—she believed that I should not focus on returning to college and it would be better to set more "realistic goals."

Upon hearing her evaluation, I became furious. I thought, *Who is she to tell me what I can or cannot do? She does not even know me. I am a very determined and stubborn person!* I believe it was at that very moment that I decided that I would somehow, someday, return to college.

It took me a long time and a lot of hard work, but I finally returned to the University of Texas in the fall of 1983—a year and a half after almost dying. The next few years in Austin were very difficult for me, but I truly believe that in order to see beauty in life, you have to experience some unpleasantness. Maybe I have experienced too much unpleasantness, but I believe in living each day to the fullest, and doing the very best I can.

Each new day was busy and full, for besides attending classes at the university, I underwent therapy three to five days each week at Brackenridge Hospital. If this were not enough, I flew to Houston every other weekend to work with Tom Williams, a trainer and executive who worked for many colleges and professional teams, and also had helped many injured athletes, such as Earl Campbell and Eric Dickerson.

Through Tom I learned: "Nothing is impossible and never, never give up or quit."

He echoed the same words and sentiment of a prominent neurosurgeon from Houston, Dr. Alexander Gol. Dr. Gol was a close personal friend of my parents who drove to Austin with my family that traumatic February morning. Over many months, I received many opinions from different therapists and doctors, but it was Dr. Gol who told my family to take one day at a time, for no matter how bad the situation looked, no one knew for certain what the brain could do.

Early during my therapy, my father kept repeating to me one of his favorite sayings. It could have been written by Tom or Dr. Gol, and I have repeated it almost every day since being hurt.

"Mile by mile it's a trial; yard by yard it's hard; but inch by inch it's a cinch."

I thought of those words, and I thought of Dr. Gol, Tom, my family, and Sharon, who believed so strongly in me as I climbed the steps to receive my diploma from the Dean of Liberal Arts at the University of Texas on a bright sunny afternoon in June 1986. Excitement and pride filled my heart as I heard the dean announce that I had graduated with "highest honors" (grade point average of 3.885), been elected to Phi Beta Kappa, and chosen as one of the twelve Dean's Distinguished Graduates out of 1,600 in the College of Liberal Arts. The overwhelming emotions and feelings that I experienced at that very moment, when most of the audience gave me a standing ovation, I felt would never again be matched in my life—not even when I graduated with a master's degree in social work or when I became employed full time at the Texas Pain and Stress Center. But I was wrong.

On May 24, 1987, I realized that nothing could ever match the joy I felt as Sharon and I were married. Sharon—my high school sweetheart of nine years—had always stood by me, through good and bad times. To me, Sharon is my miracle, my diamond in a world filled with problems, hurt, and pain. It was Sharon who dropped out of school when I was hurt so she could be at my side constantly. She never wavered or gave up on me.

It was her faith and love that pulled me through so many dark days. While other nineteen-year-old girls were going to parties and enjoying life, Sharon devoted her life to my recovery. That, to me, is the true definition of love. After our beautiful wedding, I continued working part-time at the Pain Center and completed my work for a master's degree while Sharon worked as a speech pathologist at a local hospital. We were extremely happy, but even happier when we learned Sharon was pregnant.

On July 11, 1990, at 12:15 a.m., Sharon woke me with the news: "We need to go to the hospital. My water just broke." I couldn't help think how ironic it was that my life almost ended in a convenience store, and now on the date 7/11, we were about to bring a new life into this world. This time it was my turn to help Sharon as she had helped me over those past years. Sharon was having contractions about every two minutes, and each time she needed to have her lower back massaged. Since she was in labor for fifteen hours, that meant 450 massages. It was well worth every bit of pain in my fingers because at 3:10 p.m. Sharon and I experienced the birth of our beautiful daughter, Shawn Elyse Segal! Tears of joy and happiness came to my eyes as our healthy, alert, wonderful daughter entered this world. It truly was a beautiful picture that was etched in my mind forever as she lay in her mother's arms just minutes after her birth. At that moment I thanked God for blessing us with the greatest miracle of all.

– Michael Jordan Segal

Michael Jordan Segal is a social worker at Memorial Hermann Hospital working primarily with patients and families in the Neuro Trauma Intensive Care Unit. He married his high school sweetheart, Sharon, and together have a daughter, Shawn. Mike has had national recognition about his "miraculous" comeback after being shot in the head as an innocent bystander to a robbery. In addition to his work at the hospital, he is an author (with several of his stories being published in anthologies, ezines, and newsletters) and a sought after inspirational speaker. For more information please visit www.InspirationByMike.com or call Sterling International Speakers Bureau, toll free, at 1-877-226-1003.

The Most Glorious Vocation

On a hot, muggy August afternoon, the world seemed to go on just as usual. But for me it was anything but usual. Seventy-two hours earlier, my father had had a near-death experience when he suddenly stopped breathing. Now, he sat in the intensive care unit surrounded by machines, having just coming off a ventilator. He had survived, but if it were to happen again, we had to know what he wanted.

My dad was soon diagnosed with terminal lung cancer. We learned that, while chemotherapy could possibly put the cancer into remission, it was incurable. His prognosis was six months. We had all cried. Watching him lose his hair and then begin suffering was heartbreaking. But along with the pain and tears there was such beauty.

During the last two-and-a half years of his life Dad taught me how to fight and when to surrender. He taught me to trust. He trusted not only in God but in his wife as well. Toward the end, Mom would sit by his hospital bedside, sleeping most nights in a hospital recliner. She truly showed me the sacredness of the sacrament of matrimony and what "in sickness and in health" meant. Dad trusted in her and the commitment they had made to each other forty-eight years ago. It was evident that he was so grateful for her love and devotion just by the way he looked at her.

As the months passed into years, we all knew how precious each day was. But now, we had to face the inevitable, and Dad had a decision to make. Did he want to be resuscitated again?

As Mom started talking to him about his wishes, I wasn't sure if I could keep my composure. It was so difficult for her to ask him. She started and stopped several times but, finally, after several deep breaths and many tears, she asked what he wanted regarding resuscitation. Dad grew quiet. The minutes seemed like hours as I pushed back a lump in my throat that held back the tears. I began to focus intently on the small wooden cross hanging in the center of the wall "Please God, help me be strong," I prayed silently, over and over again. Then Dad broke the silence with his old, familiar voice. Tears glistened in his eyes as he looked lovingly at Mom and slowly said, "I don't want to be a burden to you, but I don't want to leave you."

My mom gently reached for his hand and stroked his hair back. "Jerry, let's think of it as you are going on one of the most glorious vacations ever, and I will catch up to you later." With a simple nod of the head, my dad accepted this, and as tears streamed down our faces, a sense of peace filled the room. His charts were marked, and he wore a band around his wrist designating him as a "do not resuscitate" patient. Even with this, he kept up his hope and worked diligently for weeks, trying to regain strength to return home. He was anxious for Thursday, September 6, to arrive since this was the date the doctors had set for him to go home. He proudly let his many visitors know that he would be going home then.

After their nightly ritual of praying together, Mom left his hospital room to go home and make the final preparations for his homecoming the next day. Shortly after midnight, the phone startled Mom awake. A nurse from the hospital called to tell her that Dad was being taken to the emergency room because of difficulty breathing. With urgency in her voice, the nurse told Mom to come to the hospital right away.

Mom arrived to find Dad wide awake. He had been asking for Mary, my mom, over and over again. The nurse advised my mom that he had minutes, maybe hours left. Mom stroked his hair back one last time, and with love in her voice, she courageously said, "Jerry, it's OK. Go ahead. It's time to take that vacation."

A tear fell down his cheek, and he closed his eyes. He had surrendered. His fight was over. On that September day, he had been so diligently preparing for his return home, but instead he was taken to his eternal home. He now waits for his loved ones to join him on the most glorious vacation ever with our Lord Jesus.

— Susan Babcock

Susan Babcock lives in Iowa with her husband and three children. She has been a stay-at-home mom for the past thirteen years. Susan also teaches religious education and serves as a Eucharistic minister to shut-ins. She credits the example of faith and devotion she learned from her parents for helping her to continue to grow in her faith.

Chapter 6

Family Matters

The "Imperfect" Storm

I'm what you might call a weather geek. I am *passionate* about the weather. This passion for weather began at an early age. When I was growing up in White River Junction, Vermont, my schoolmates would call me up for their weather forecasts. "Hey, Jim. It's supposed to snow. Will there be enough to cancel school tomorrow?" In junior high I was a budding meteorologist and did not even know it till the day my dad told me that I needed to study the weather because that was all I ever talked about.

I get ribbed about it, but the fact is, everyone worries about the weather. As long as humans have been on this earth, we have been trying to predict it and control it. I believe that is what makes it so fascinating. I just never thought that my life would ever be more unpredictable than the weather.

I landed my dream job right out of college—working for The Weather Channel (TWC), a budding cable network out of Atlanta. That is where I met the two people who would have a huge influence on my life: my mentor and friend, the late Mr. John Hope, and my wife-to-be, Tamra (Tammy). John was our "hurricane expert" for many years. He was everybody's grandfather, and when he had something to say, you listened. I will never forget the day John told me that my tropical updates stunk. I was crushed, but that drove me to become the best communicator, teacher, and meteorologist that I could be. I miss him dearly.

Tammy was director of affiliate sales, and a TWC veteran.

She caught my attention immediately at our annual TWC picnic and she passed the ultimate test ... she was a skier! Like me, she was passionate about her job and a fireball of energy. Along with her great skiing ability, she played tennis, was involved with her church, and did many other activities. Maybe best of all, she never got bored or relied on me to stay busy. Whether it was a blinding snowstorm or a major hurricane, she understood that I needed to get in it to be happy. I proposed to Tammy during a snowstorm in Colorado, and we married in Vermont in the fall of 1990, at the peak of leaf season. Our daughter, Christina, came along in July of 1993 and Ben followed in July of 1995. Having the kids hardly slowed Tamra down at all.

In 1997, shortly after Ben's second birthday, when Tammy noticed that her hand was twitching and her walk had become tentative, she said, "I must have pinched a nerve from carrying Ben around so much." She made an appointment with our friend and chiropractor, Dr. Robert Schlampp. He told her to see a neurologist. "So he can help me out with my pinched nerve?" she inquired.

"No, Tammy, I think something else is wrong." He interviewed neurologists on her behalf and got two new opinions that yielded a different extended outlook: a one hundred percent chance of Parkinson's Disease!

Tammy wasn't even forty. Wasn't Parkinson's something that old people got? The doctors tried to put a good spin on it. "If you're going to get this disease," one of them said, "you couldn't have picked a better time to get it. Breakthroughs are happening every day. We could be very close to a cure." Tammy dove into her new challenge: learning everything she could about Parkinson's. She became active in fundraising and advocacy efforts of the Parkinson's community and lobbied her legislators in Washington, D.C. Having been so active all of her life, the reality of her condition hit hard at the first Parkinson's convention she attended. For one thing, seeing the condition of others fighting this same monster was frightening. Another harsh reality was that—unlike telecommunications industry conventions—there were no tennis or golf tournaments at Parkinson's conventions.

Over the next couple of years, she understood why. On a bad day, she could not even brush Christina's hair. But even when I did not know which way this storm was going to go, Tamra knew how to handle this situation. "God's never given me more than I could handle before," my wife declared.

Life was insanely complicated at times, but we did our best to get through it. But then, at an age when most kids are tearing around like little tornadoes, Ben was barely walking; Christina had regular ear infections. When we had time to breathe a little, we realized something was not right with our kids. A genetic counselor did some blood work on Tammy, the kids, and me. This storm started out as a little blip on the radar screen, but combined with our current storm it could create the Imperfect Storm. It turned out to be Fragile X Syndrome, a disability both our children have been diagnosed with. Fragile X is an inherited disease that shows up with a variety of physical and behavioral characteristics more noticeable in males due to the fact that we have only one X chromosome, and women have two. Fragile X symptoms vary from mild learning disabilities to severe mental retardation. Ben and Christina both suffered from it, but because the syndrome affects males more strongly than females, Christina's had escaped notice until just last year.

Because of the autistic-type behavior with Fragile X, if we do not prepare the kids for what we are going to do or how we are going to spend a day, the consequences can be a disaster. On the other hand, the elated joys of the smallest accomplishments and the unconditional love I receive from our children are my piece of heaven here on earth.

Within three years, our lives had gone from clear skies to dark and ominous. No hurricane, no blizzard, no tornado, and no flood were even remotely close to the never-ending storm that

I was in. This storm does not clear up after a few days of bad weather; I cannot rebuild anything; and worst of all, I cannot control it or forecast the outcome.

One day, I was watching Tammy and Christina play with Christina's Barbies. Christina loves it when her mom can help dress them. Tammy was fumbling with the buttons on one of the doll's jackets.

"Here, Mom," said Christina. "Those buttons are small. I'll do it."

Tammy looked up at me. Our eyes met. *Don't worry*, they seemed to say. *We'll get through this.*

I can't begin to describe the transformation of my wife since the day of her diagnosis—even though I still wish it would just dissipate. But it is through this dreadful disease that her true strengths have been revealed—and revealed to so many. Never a day goes by where she does not help a friend in need. The weaknesses of Parkinson's are overshadowed by the strengths in character and compassion for others. She is the *rock* of our house.

"For you have been a stronghold to the poor, a stronghold to the needy in his distress, a shelter from the storm and a shade from the heat" (Is 25:4).

I won't say the sky is always sunny because it isn't. There will be adversity, but more importantly, there will be heroism, triumph, and hope. How do I know? Trust me. I'm a weatherman.

– Jim Cantore

Jim Cantore is a veteran storm chaser for The Weather Channel in Atlanta.

Blessed and Broken

The morning I left St. Mary's Hospital without my baby, my seventh child, I wept the whole way. It was beyond my comprehension to be leaving without my daughter.

I was anxious to get to Children's Hospital, where my new daughter had been transported, but first I had to stop at home to see the other children. Aaron and the children had put up signs on the front of the house: *It's a Girl!* A message that should have filled me with joy only compounded my pain. My little girl was born, but not in my arms where she belonged.

The trip to the hospital took only twenty minutes, but it seemed endless. Once in the NICU, the first thing one notices is the quiet. One would expect a room full of babies to be noisy. Instead, there is stillness. Those whose breathing is assisted with ventilators cannot cry. Many are sedated to diminish their suffering. The stillness, so unnatural, is unexpected, and harsh, and unrelenting.

I trembled with anticipation and fear, overcome with longing for my daughter. I was afraid to touch her, afraid I would harm her or disconnect a wire. She looked like someone else's child. I normally have strapping ten-pounders who cry lustily and nurse eagerly. This was my baby, my Celeste. I took the time to draw her close, to touch her gently, to kiss her tiny head. I went home that night without her, of course. I recalled that Jesus had given me His own mother at the foot of the cross. "Then he said to the disciple, 'Behold your mother'" (Jn 19:27). Jesus spoke not only to St. John, but to me—and to Celeste. I left Celeste in Mary's care. She would not abandon my baby, even as I knew I must, in body if not in spirit.

Celeste needed prayer, and if I could not be at her bedside twenty-four hours a day, if I could not hold her and nurse her and tend to her as I should, I would get those prayers for her. So that first night after I had met Celeste, I wrote about her.

Hello everyone,

First of all, thank you so much for your prayers for our new daughter! She is getting more beautiful each day and we are already feeling so blessed having her in our life.

Celeste is healthy and perfectly formed in most ways, but she does have a rare heart defect called Ebstein's Anomaly (which is a malformation of a heart valve) and two holes in her heart. She is also possibly battling an intestinal problem. She is not in immediate danger, but it is very scary for us. What the doctors are telling us is "wait and see," which we are hearing as "wait and PRAY!" We are hoping you will all join us in doing that for Celeste.

We know that prayer is powerful, and we are asking for your help.

"God Who is mighty has done great things, and Holy is His Name!" I know there is a reason that has been going through my head since my labor began. God is already doing great things with Celeste's life. We will keep you posted.

Thank you and God bless you,
Cathy and Aaron

Our days began to form a pattern. Visiting Celeste was our priority, but we had six other children, five of them at home. The addition of another child, no matter how special, did not diminish the needs of the others. We were torn between our desire to be with the baby and the very real importance of maintaining some kind of normalcy at home.

We arrived at the NICU that day hoping that she would be home soon. Instead, we held her in our arms and tried to feed her a bottle, and watched something go very wrong. She turned pale and started to perspire.

A technician took a blood sample and made a grim announcement: She was acidotic, which meant she was not getting enough oxygen. "Bag her!" the nurse shouted. It wasn't working. "We need to intubate her *now*," the nurse said. I offered up a quick prayer, and immediately felt a maternal presence. Mary was with me, in a very real way. I asked her to take care of my baby. With that we were quickly ushered out while they prepared to put her on a ventilator.

We wept in the hall outside her room. The nurse assured me that the doctors were taking care of Celeste, doing everything they needed to do. The hospital chaplain was there to pray with us, if we desired. Her words were balm: "Would you like to pray?"

Her faith tradition was different from ours, but at that moment we were simply brothers and sisters in the Lord. As we talked, I continued to weep. She asked if we were believers. We nodded, and she had another question. "Do you trust Him?" I nodded again. "Then why are you crying?"

It was said with such kindness, not at all harsh. Why indeed? If I trusted God to do only the best for Celeste, then I should not cry. But my human heart was afraid. In my e-mail that night I wrote: *We know that God has a plan for Celeste's life and that His will is perfect. We know that she will glorify Him in a unique way, and that "all things work together for the good of those who love Him." Despite all our pain, we are so happy to have our Celeste.*

As our requests for support spread out through the Web, prayers rained down on us. Daily we received e-mails confirming that our need was being shared with many. In our case, the prayers of others became an invisible net that sustained us.

It became clear that Celeste was touching many lives. Members of our parish and the homeschooling community to which we belonged prayed faithfully and offered meals and conversation. Thanks to a friend in our church family whom I have known since high school, I heard from classmates from around the country. Co-workers of my husband's shared Celeste's needs with friends and family, and a network of prayer support developed throughout our community. Relatives in Poland prayed, including a cousin of Aaron's, a priest who asked his congregation to remember Celeste. Churches of various denominations put her on prayer lists. Several orders of nuns in different locales interceded for her. I heard later that one mother superior in a cloistered order read my e-mail updates to the sisters as they ate their evening meal.

One morning, I was visiting Celeste when a woman I had never seen before entered her room. She identified herself as a doctor—a dentist, in fact—who worked downstairs. *A dentist*, I thought. *How odd!* Celeste didn't even have any teeth! She was receiving my e-mails and wanted to meet the child for whom she had been praying. I was amazed and heartened.

Hospital staff had introduced me to several mothers of children who had undergone heart surgery. I was attracted at once to the mother of a little boy, age six, who'd had a heart transplant as an infant. It *was* surprising to discover she had been praying for me before we met—her husband belonged to a work-related prayer group and had been receiving my e-mails and sharing them there. Amazing. Like a pebble in a pond, little Celeste's life was sending ripples into the world.

The days in the NICU lengthened into weeks, the weeks into months. Each day we visited Celeste and cared for our family as best we could. Time kept going in the world around us, but in the NICU there was one constant. There was suffering.

I convinced myself that she knew we were there, that she sensed our moods. I did not want her to ever feel despair or fear. I did not want our sorrow to consume her. The nurses confirmed this belief, saying that their experiences told them the babies with the most pleasant parents fared the best. Wanting to do everything we could for Celeste, we smiled at her bedside. We told funny stories. Aaron sang to her every day.

On July 12, she looked the same as before, but nothing was is the same.

The resident scurried around the nurses' station, seeming to avoid me. There were nurses everywhere, doctors making rounds, interns taking notes. Everyone seemed to be moving very slowly, very softly, and avoiding me. I asked whomever I saw to find out the results of the previous night's MRI but they all stared at me blankly.

Finally, I learned the results of the MRI: "Profound brain damage, insufficient growth, multiple strokes—not a transplant candidate."

No transplant.

No transplant.

No transplant.

I headed to the NICU, not quite sure what I would do when I got there. My daughter was going to die, of that I was sure. I needed to talk to someone who knew me.

I maintained my composure until I walked through the double doors. I saw Sunshine, who was also awaiting a heart transplant for her baby. Her eyes were wild with fear. If my baby could die, so could hers. She tried to comfort me, but I knew it was over for us, that our families no longer shared the bond of a common solution.

We had a party for Celeste's four-month birthday.

There was no cake and no balloons, but there were plenty of children, which is what parties are all about anyway. Celeste was beautiful in pink.

For the first time, ever, all seven of my children were in the same room. We took lots of pictures, and smiled and sang. There was much laughter, even authentic joy. Today, we had our baby girl, Celeste, and are together.

Later that day, I e-mailed friends and family:

I have a few very important things to tell you all now. First of all, I do not want any of you to feel that your prayers have not been answered. God is always faithful, and He always gives us what is best for us. Celeste has done so much in her four months here. She has touched so many people and will continue to do so from heaven! Our hearts are breaking as we think about letting her go, but she

*belongs to Him anyway. Do not despair! Please keep praying, about
everything in your lives! God loves us so much. He has blessed us
so greatly through Celeste. And your prayers have worked miracles.
Celeste may not live, but it is a miracle that we are surviving this.
That is due to those prayers.*

*I also want to express that in no way are we basing any decision
on "quality of life" for Celeste. I have never liked that phrase. We
are not ending her life. We are not letting her go because she is not
perfect. We would care for her no matter what, and we know ALL
people are beautiful reflections of God's perfection, no matter what
defect they may have. We were very careful to consider the teaching
of our Church on this, a teaching we believe to be true and beautiful.
Those of you who know us well know we are strongly pro- life. But
to prolong the life of one whom God is calling home is humanistic,
not Christian. We know that sometimes God calls His children
home when they are tiny. Thinking about this gave me more peace.
If Celeste were ninety years old, we would not be doubtful about
anything. We would say she had a good life and that we should not
put her through unnecessary pain. The same is true for our little
baby. She has had a good life. She has never offended God with the
tiniest sin. She is perfect and pure and wonderful. What a blessing.*

*So now please pray for a peaceful passing for our dear Celeste. It
is difficult to say how long this may take; of course, it could be hours
or days. Once again it is in God's hands. You know how much we
need your prayers now. Thank you for being there for us.*

When we arrived at the hospital, we bathed our baby girl.
She grimaced, as she always did, as we lathered her hair and
rinsed her chubby body. We dressed her in her baptismal gown.
She was beautiful.

The hospital room was tiny, but we crammed our whole family
and several close friends inside to witness her confirmation. Lauren,
her sister and godmother, held her while Father anointed her. She

was sedated, but when he told her to open her eyes and receive the gifts of the Holy Spirit, she obeyed. A hush fell on the room.

As the sacrament was completed, we knew that Celeste was a fully incorporated member of the Body of Christ. She was sinless and pure, and would enter heaven immediately upon her death.

Friends and family said their good-byes to her. We, with the help of hospice nurses, made molds of her hands and feet and cut locks of her hair and took photographs. Finally, the others left so we could have her to ourselves. We dressed her in a pink terry cloth sleeper. The nurse gently removed her ventilator tube. Such a tiny tube, so easily removed, had kept my daughter alive for so long. And now it was gone.

All of the tubes and wires were removed, the monitors silenced, and for the very first time, I held my daughter up to my cheek, her head on my shoulder.

Rocking with her daddy, she was beautiful to us, but truly not very pretty. Her color was bad, and she looked battered, almost bruised. We were completely enraptured with her.

I felt a desperate need to be alone with her, so Aaron graciously left. A pain surged through me in waves that I did not expect. She was leaving me. I finally began to weep. I rocked her and whispered her name, again and again. Aaron came back in, and I felt at peace again.

She did not seem to be suffering, but we could tell she would leave us soon. Her breathing became shallow, her skin mottled. A nurse checked her heart and nodded; it would be soon. Aaron looked at me, his eyes pleading. I knew he needed to hold her, so I handed her to him. She let out a tiny breath, a gentle sigh.

She was gone, and I was overwhelmed with grief but also joy, awe, and amazement. I had seen a glimpse of heaven.

– Cathy Adamkiewicz

Cathy Adamkiewicz is a Catholic wife, mother, home-educating parent, writer, and speaker. After earning a communications degree from the University of Detroit in 1986, she dedicated herself to the creation of her life's work: her family. In her book Broken and Blessed *(Bezalel Books), she poignantly shares a message of hope and the value of a suffering life through the story of one baby girl, her daughter, Celeste, and her amazing ministry of presence. Visit www. brokenandblessed.com to order the book and to learn more about Celeste's story.*

Just Come Home

The phone rang. It was my son Mark calling from California to confirm what we suspected. My twenty-two-year-old daughter, Marie, had had a relapse back to drugs. In the eighties, when she was eighteen, she moved from Michigan to California and began her downward spiral, from alcohol to common street drugs to cocaine.

Marie lived at Mark's home for about four months. She then moved to a section of San Diego seeded with drug dealers and addicts. Mark tried everything to get her to go home and seek help. We have a very close, loving family of eleven children, most of whom still live in Michigan. Those living out-of-state touch base with us or someone else in the family every week or two. Calls from Marie came further and further apart. Mark did not say anything because he was hoping she would straighten up before we found out.

Then came the call from Mark. I knew if we did not do something quickly, we could lose her. There were two people that were our lifeline to her—Mark, her brother, and Armondo, her boyfriend, who had actually gotten completely out of drugs. Armondo still cared very much for Marie. He tried the best he could to watch over her.

I decided I would go out two weeks prior to Easter. The Saturday before I left, many of our family members went to confession to send a pure prayer to heaven. We knew the greatest help would come from God. We have close relatives in California, but I did not let anyone know I was coming so that I could devote one-hundred percent of my time trying to persuade Marie to get help.

I must admit I had a secret desire to do two things if the circumstances were different. The first was to go to the Crystal Cathedral and see *The Glory of Easter*, a play about the passion of Christ. The second was to go to St. Maria Goretti Church in

Scottsdale, Arizona. But our mission to get Marie was the most important, so I put these thoughts out of my mind.

I arrived in San Diego on Monday. I was anxious to get started as quickly as possible. Mark thought it best if we went to Marie's in the evening, about 8:00 p.m. She was angry that I had just showed up. Armondo and Mark left us alone to talk. We sat on the couch and talked and cried. She looked so thin to me, but her skin, teeth, and hair were strangely in good condition. Many people on crack loose their teeth, their hair gets thin, and their skin breaks out.

All the children in her neighborhood loved Marie, and they often came to the door for her. People of the community, of different backgrounds and races, gathered together as a family, replacing the family and friends they had left behind. I wondered how this happened to her since her family cared so much for one another. Marie told me terrible and sad stories about things that had happened in the months since she had been there. A little boy had been struck by a car in front of her house. She heard the screech, came running out, and the boy died in her arms. Another time a man put a gun to her head in an attempt to steal her car, a car she had stopped making payments on and soon after was repossessed. She said that she really believed in her guardian angel because she seemed protected so often.

I asked her to come back to Mark's with me. I made it clear that if she did not cooperate, I intended to move into the area. I was sure she did not want her mother hanging around. She looked a little strung out to me and probably needed time to digest the fact that I was there. She would not come with me that night but promised she would come over the next day.

The next day, Tuesday, I waited anxiously for her to call or come over. Finally, around 9:00 p.m., when I was about to give up, she and Armondo arrived. I ordered Chinese food for everyone. It amazed me to watch Marie eat. I did not know anyone as thin as she was could eat that much. After several hours of eating and talking, Marie laid down on the couch and fell asleep. Armondo decided to leave without telling her. Mark had a great idea. He said that I could use his truck and take her as far away as I could the next day. Maybe just being out of that environment would give her time to come to her senses.

Wednesday morning arrived. Marie woke up about 10:00 a.m. and agreed to go to her sister Gloria's house with me, about sixty miles away in San Clemente. It occurred to me that we were close to the Crystal Cathedral. I asked Gloria and Marie if they would like to go see *The Glory of Easter*? They agreed! Marie slept through most of the play. I was thrilled and grateful that we were there together. After the play we went back to Gloria's house and spent the night. Thursday arrived. Could it be possible that Marie would agree to go see her brother John, who was six hundred miles away in Scottsdale, Arizona? Once again I got lucky. We were on our way.

Every day brought its own little miracles. Friday morning, I suggested we get up early and go to Mass at St. Maria Goretti. The tears just rolled out of my eyes before Holy Communion. I thought again how good God is, how He managed to work in the very two things I wanted to do. After Mass, we went to the gift shop, bought rosaries, and had them blessed by Father Jack Spalding, the pastor. Marie felt much peace there.

Friday at noon we headed back to Mark's. The ride back was completely different from the ride there. Marie talked to me for hours. It was a time of baring our souls. I felt there was such honesty between us. This was the first day I felt I was with my daughter, as I knew her from the past. Marie agreed to go back home with me on Monday. I thought all was well.

When we got back to Mark's place, Armondo was there. The four of us talked for several hours. We continued to bare our souls, and everyone expressed how they felt. As our conversation wound down, Marie said she had to pick up her things at her house and say good-bye to her friends. This set off a red light, but

I could not stop her. Mark owned an old purple Mustang that he was working on to sell. He told Armondo he could use it to take Marie, but to bring it back in the morning.

I spent Saturday morning waiting for a call. It was nearing 2:00 p.m., and I was getting nervous. Mark was ready to go over to their house and check on his car. I put a rosary around my neck like a necklace, wearing it on the outside of my tee shirt. I felt a sense of protection. When we arrived at the house only to find no one home, we went to an abandoned apartment where many addicts hung out, but again, we could not find her. We spotted the purple Mustang and hot-wired it. Armondo then called to report that Marie had left her house immediately the night before, looking for a quick fix. After going without anything for five days, she was really feeling a need for something. He said it was very unusual that no one in that part of San Diego could find any drugs; the county was dry. Apparently, there was some kind of a drug war going on, and everything was shut down. All things are possible with God. He also said that when Mark and I were at the apartment building that afternoon, we were watched from the upper-floor windows as we picked up the Mustang. Marie and some of her friends noticed that my rosary glistened in the sun. Her friends said they hoped her mother would be leaving town soon, taking her rosary with her.

We wondered how to get Marie back now. It was late Saturday afternoon. Our tickets home were for 12:20 p.m. on Monday. We had one day left. Around midnight Mark and I went back to Marie's house. Armondo was there, but Marie was gone. We decided to drive back to the abandoned apartment. There were people hanging around the corners, looking like zombies. We wanted to drive around the apartment, so we went down a dark, narrow alley in back of the building. There we saw ten or twelve men standing in a group. I was frightened. Further down the alley, we realized it was a dead end so we had to back out past them again.

Just as we passed the gang for the second time, I saw Marie

come out of the apartment with a group of people, headed by a young man with a big club in his hand. I called out to Marie and pleaded with her to come back with us. The man stepped forward as if he were going to attack us. Marie interceded and said, "Stop! That's my mother and brother." She then told me that if I did not leave her alone, she would not come home with me on Monday. She was just spending a last day or two with her friends. Mark and I had no choice but to leave without Marie. That night I cried my heart out.

On Sunday morning, we went to church. In the afternoon, Mark and I thought we would go back to her house and try again. Mark was angry about the night before. He said, "He had a club. I'll bring a bigger club, or maybe I'll take a knife or a gun." I replied, "No, we have the only weapon we'll need," and I took my rosary.

Armondo told us that Marie was still searching for some drugs over at the apartment. We went to the apartment and went inside. We were met by the same young man who'd had the club the night before. I asked him if he had seen Marie. He said he didn't know where she was, but we did not believe him. We left without finding Marie and went back to talk to Armondo, who suggested that we wait until midnight since she probably would not go with us now even if we found her.

Sometime after 10:00 p.m., Armondo said that if there were still no drugs available, maybe by morning she might give in and come home with me. His plan was to follow her everywhere that night. At 8:00 a.m. Monday, Armondo called to tell us he was in jail. While he was trying to keep an eye on Marie, she became angry and told him to leave her alone. Two police officers heard them and asked my daughter if there was a problem. She told them that she wanted Armondo to stop following her. Half an hour later, the same policemen found them still arguing. They ran a check on Armondo and arrested him for an unpaid traffic violation. We found that to be strange because Marie had two or three tickets she had not paid. Mark told Armondo he would take care of him later, but right now we had to concentrate on Marie.

That gave us an idea. If Marie would not come with us, perhaps we could have her arrested for unpaid tickets. At least she would be out of the bad environment and with another drug-free week, maybe she would be ready to come to her senses.

We arrived at Marie's and could see through the mail slot that she was sleeping on the couch. "Marie, get up!" I called. She later said it was like a flash back from school days as she got up half asleep and opened the door. Seeing us, she became angry. Marie had made up her mind that she did not want to go back to Michigan. She decided her life was with these people and it was her mission to stay and help them.

I told her that I loved her and wanted her to come home with me. She told me she loved me but she was not going. Meanwhile, in the other room, Mark and Gloria proceeded with the plan to call the police. It was about 10:30 a.m. One of the neighbors came to the house to see what was going on. Marie overheard Mark tell the neighbor she should leave because the police would soon be there. With that, Marie called out and said that if that's the way we wanted it, that was all right with her. At least she would get some rest in jail. I broke down and cried. At that point, I gave up all hope of her coming home with me.

As Marie walked out the bedroom, the police arrived. Two young officers came through the living room. They began to question her as she walked back to the bedroom to put on her shoes. Mark sat back on his heels, put his head in his hands and cried. The three of us gave up all hope. Suddenly, one of the officers came out of the other bedroom and said, "Marie, I'm sorry, but I'm going to have to arrest you for possession of rock" (the slang term for crack cocaine). We all looked up in shock!

The officer walked into the front room holding a large rock in his hand—an actual fieldstone. It was a joke! Suddenly, laughter burst out, cutting all the tension. Then the other officer turned around and said, "Marie, why don't you go home with your mom?"

To our amazement she answered, "All right." We could hardly believe it. They never even mentioned the tickets. I thanked them profusely.

"All in a day's work, ma'am," they said. It was like something right out of the movies.

Once Marie made up her mind to go home with us, the struggle was over. We went to Mark's to pick up my luggage and still had enough time to stop for lunch before getting dropped off at the airport. One the plane ride home, Marie said that there was a saying back in the neighborhood when someone had some crack that "you gotta break me off some of that good stuff." She looked at my rosary and said, "You gotta break me off some of that good stuff."

Marie spent one year in a rehabilitation program at Dawn Farms. She has been sober for close to fifteen years now, and we are very happy and grateful to see what a wonderful person she has become.

– Margaret Williams

Margaret Williams was named Mother of Year for Right to Life -"Life Span" in 1995. She is a widow with eleven children, twenty-nine grandchildren, and three great grandchildren. Margaret stays busy with church activities and with many organizations such as Right to Life, the Evangelization Team, and Emmanuel. She has also been instrumental in a number of devotions going strong for two decades such as a First Saturday devotion at the Monastery of the Blessed Sacrament, a Rosary group every Wednesday in her home, and a Eucharistic adoration group every Friday at her parish.

God Hears a Mother's Prayers

Pedro Cumba's first brush with death came in 1995 when a rival drug gang robbed him. "They pushed me down the basement steps and made me lay face down on the floor," Cumba said. "He went to shoot me in the back of the head, but the gun didn't go off."

Pedro managed to get away, unharmed, but was not yet frightened away from the drug habit that would consume twenty of his forty-eight years of life. His second brush with death would come soon after, when his home was broken into one night. Cumba was doing drugs in the living room with his friends. "I was whacked over the back of the head with a gun, tied up, and thrown in a closet." One of the assailants put a pillow up to the closet door and started shooting but Cumba was able to wriggle himself into the corner of the closet and escaped all five bullets.

"When I got out of that one, I was telling everyone how lucky I was, but I knew in my gut it wasn't luck. It was God."

He also knew exactly who was pleading with God for his life—his mother. "I'm sure that it was her prayers to God that saved my life. I think she spent every day on her knees praying for me."

Cruz Maria Cumba came to the U.S. from Puerto Rico. With her husband, Pedro Juan, they raised three sons. Pedro, the oldest, was five when the family moved from New York City to Philadelphia. He graduated from a Catholic high school, married at nineteen, fathered two children, and was divorced seven years later. Pedro became involved in the drug culture that would hold him captive for the next twenty years. During the worst of those years, he lost touch with his mother, even though she never stopped praying for him. She often tried to call and came to his door, but Cumba would not answer.

Sometimes, his mother would leave a plate of food outside his door. "It would really hurt to watch her walk away," Cumba said. "But I just could not face her the way I was." One day his mother left a letter at his door. "She said how much she loved me and that she knew I wasn't well. No matter what I was doing, I would always be her son and she would always be my mother. She said, 'My address is still the same, and my phone number is the same. You'll always have a home here.'"

Cruz Maria's unconditional love had a powerful effect on her son. Even seven years later, just talking about it choked him up with emotion. "I hung the letter up on the wall and I would look at it every day," he said. It wore on him until finally, one day, he picked up the phone and called her.

They reconciled and started going to church together and even to prayer meetings. By now, Cumba realized everything that had happened to him was an opportunity from God to turn his life around. "But I still had one foot in the world," he said. "I'd leave church and several days later, I'd go back to doing drugs. This happened for about a year. I was going to the prayer group, but I was still messing up."

Then one night, the leader of the prayer group, Nancy Martinez, prayed over him. Toward the end of the prayer, she said that the Lord had just revealed to her that Cumba had twice confronted death. "That really freaked me out," Cumba said. "How could she know this? Nobody knew that except the people who were with me when it happened."

Martinez warned him that he was about to face death a third time and told him to give his heart to the Lord without delay.

The very next weekend, after a night of drugs, Cumba woke up with a splitting headache. "I looked in the mirror and one eye was completely shut and my mouth was turned funny. I thought it was from the air conditioning."

He walked around for a week in this condition before collapsing in someone's car. The emergency room doctor told him that he had suffered a brain aneurism. One vessel had exploded, and another vessel had a bubble on it the size of a dime. "If that one explodes," the doctor told Cumba, "I can't save you." The only hope was an emergency surgery, but Cumba wanted no part of it. He attempted to leave the hospital but the doctor told him, "If you walk out of here, you're going to die."

"I burst into tears and went into the bathroom of the emergency room. I had seven rocks of crack cocaine in my pocket, and instead of throwing them down the toilet like I should have done, I decided to end my life right there by smoking all seven rocks back-to-back."

He smoked them, but he did not die. "There I was trying to kill myself and I still could not die." At some point, he realized that maybe God did not want him to die because He had something for him to do. Maybe it was something worth living for.

"OK," he told the Lord, "I'm going to put my life in your hands. If it's your will that I make it through the operation, if you give me a second chance, I promise I'll turn my life around."

The surgery took almost ten hours. When he awoke, the first sound he heard was that of his mother praying with friends from the prayer group who had gathered around his bed. The left side of his face was paralyzed and he was blind and deaf on that side. "I was so thankful to be alive, that I did not care what I looked like." He endured months of therapy, both physical and spiritual. He became more and more convinced that God had work for him to do.

"I knew God had spared my life, and I wanted to do something for Him. I just couldn't sit and warm the pews in church. I had to get out there and touch lives the way He touched mine."

That's exactly what he did. After regaining his sight and hearing, which doctors never expected to happen, he started singing in the choir at the prayer group. Then, he learned how to play bass guitar. From there, he joined the Spirit of the Lord street ministry that reaches out to the very people Cumba knew best—troubled souls on drugs. Headed by Nestali Montes, the ministry sets up their band on drug-infested corners, plays gospel music, and preaches the word of God. Prostitutes and drug addicts have fallen on their knees right in the street and given their hearts to Jesus Christ. Cumba tell them, "If you just open your heart to Jesus, there's nothing He can't forgive."

Cumba also conducts a monthly prayer service with music for boys. At the end of the meetings, anyone who wants to accept Christ can come forward and turns his life over to the Lord. Cumba offers himself as a witness to the unconditional love of God that came to him through the heart of his mother. It is the grace that saved his life.

— Susan Brinkmann

Susan Brinkmann's biography appears after "Never Say Never" in chapter five.

Full Circle

I remember the feeling like it was yesterday. The teacher would call on me, and I would panic. My palms would become damp with sweat, and my throat would tighten. I'd take a deep breath and tell myself to calm down, but anxiety would force its way up. The eyes of the other students seemed to bore a hole through me, watching and waiting for the answer that would not—could not—come. A severe stuttering problem held me hostage for most of my school years, all the way through much of college. When put together with a personality that today would be dubbed attention deficit hyperactive disorder, I had the makings of a social disaster.

Grades ranging from failing to lackluster filled my report cards. With marks like those, teachers instinctively scribbled the letter "D" into the box for "Uses Time Wisely." But they knew nothing of how I used my time. I could study for days and still get a "D" on an exam. I would take in the activity around me all at once, but focusing on one thing was a challenge. I was just a step behind everyone else. If I flunked a class during the year, I could get an "A" on it during summer school. I needed time to let things sink in. To try only to fail, to talk only to stutter, were burdens of monumental proportion to a young boy. During adolescence, it could have been a death sentence. But thankfully, through Boy Scouts, I learned leadership. As an assistant patrol leader, I could prepare and succeed at campouts and help plan meetings. I earned merit badges at my own pace and took the Boy Scout pledge to heart: to be my best, to do my duty to God and my country, and to have good character. It gave me an element of success. Between Boy Scouts, a loving family, and God, I had something to hold onto. But on the last one—God—I had a tenuous grasp of at times.

I went to a Catholic school. I learned that God loved us. Yet, if He loved me so much, why did He let me hurt so badly? I was told that if I prayed to do well on a test, God would help me. But the help did not seem to come. I prayed and pleaded that He would take away my stuttering. If only the words would not get stuck in my mouth ... if only I could speak freely and not be held prisoner by my faulty communication. But I did not get better. I knew God had to be there; I just was not sure what the deal was. Sometimes, I just ignored Him. It seemed to be what He was doing to me. Other times, I said my prayers, but I kept Him at arm's length because I did not trust that He really loved me.

I was often told that I was not applying myself. It seemed to be a catch phrase for anyone with below-average grades. So I struggled through from year to year and tried to make myself invisible when teachers asked for answers or any other vocal responses. I graduated and went to college. Since most students in my high school went to college, there was never any question in my mind that if I wanted to get a good job, the struggle needed to continue.

In a moment of soul-searching during my junior year of college, I wondered where God was in all this and where I was. English was my major and history my minor, but I also had a heavy concentration of philosophy and psychology classes. Free will and self-determination were factors I began to consider as I contemplated my stuttering. The routine was always the same—a stressful situation such as public speaking increased my nervousness and paralyzed my verbal abilities. Even consciously trying to calm myself did no good. Even in college, other students mocked and imitated me. It was a vicious cycle that fed on itself. How could I turn things around?

I finally determined that instead of hiding, I would put myself into anxiety-provoking situations. With most fears and phobias, familiarity lessons the fear. So, instead of shrinking in my seat, I raised my hand. No one was cornering me anymore. Slowly, I was able to take control, calm myself, and get the words out. I even tried out for school plays. Initially, I was placed in the chorus, where I could get by as part of a group. But by senior year, I won the leading role in *South Pacific*. I also finally mastered the skill of studying and regurgitating information for tests. By the time I graduated from Sacred Heart University in 1969, the yoke of my heavy social burdens had lifted.

I eventually met and fell in love with June, who was a nurse and the most beautiful woman I had ever seen. We soon married and had two children in quick succession.

I became a junior high teacher for six years. However, with a family to support, teaching was not cutting it, so I needed to look elsewhere. It touched me deeply when the school held an appreciation dinner and two hundred of my former students showed up. One parent told me, "You had the uncanny ability to lift up the quiet ones. I want to thank you for what you did for my son. He talks now. He gives us his opinions." Other parents said the same. I knew it had been my own disability that had given me the compassion and ability to touch these students.

I tried other jobs, including sales. During a difficult time financially, I started to turn to God again. At first, it was to blame Him once more for making my life miserable. But after a religious retreat when I was thirty-seven and the father of four, a priest helped me see that God had been with me through it all. Jesus Christ was also abandoned and betrayed by his friends. God used my pain to make me stronger. Through my pain, I overcame my weaknesses and became more compassionate towards others. Soon, my career turned around, and I built a business that reached more than $700 million in revenues.

But in the end, my struggles came full circle through the course of my fatherhood. As the father of four, two of whom were active boys, I expected that the education system would have advanced, but it is still a struggle for children who don't fit into the box. My own children never stuttered, but by high school the parent-teacher conferences were déjà vu: "He's not living up to his potential." But I knew that potential was more than what was regurgitated onto a piece of paper.

By this time, I had become a very successful businessman, motivational speaker, and author. Who would have predicted that was possible? But as a father, I realized that my children would need to make their own way in the world. I came to understand that my role was to love and encourage my children. It was my job to hug them and run interference whenever the system seemed to fail them. We can't usually beat the system, but we don't have to let the system beat us down. Part of society is labeling people like my boys and me as attention deficit hyperactivity disordered, or ADHD. In my life, I've proven that it does not have to be a disorder but an asset. My energy and ability to take in many things at a time has been a positive.

I always gave my children the message that they were valuable in and of themselves. For a time, the youngest one was put on Ritalin after an official diagnosis of ADHD. But taking a drug robbed him of who he really was. I loved my children just as God had made them. We threw the Ritalin out. During their high school years, my sons played sports and were influential in a number of ways at their schools. They took on a variety of leadership roles such as leading a successful fundraiser and having the enthusiasm and energy to get a stadium full of football fans all psyched up.

Once, when my wife and I went out to dinner, we chatted with a teenage employee who went to the local high school. When we told her who our son was, her eyes opened wide, "He's your son? He's the king of the school." My boys did not let their academic challenges get the best of them.

In retrospect, that is what Christ did with the apostles. They were losers in the face of society. An outside observer probably would have picked Judas as the one most likely to succeed. Peter, the hot-headed fisherman who denied Christ three times would not be the man of choice the way society judges. But I've come to understand that God sees things differently. Our heavenly Father sees our true value and potential. As an earthly father I was given the grace to see the value in my own children and to help them understand that they are never alone because Dad and God will always be in their corner.

— Chuck Piola

Dubbed "The King of Cold Calls" by Inc. *magazine, Chuck Piola is described as a corporate leader. A native of Waterbury, Connecticut, Piola graduated from Sacred Heart University in 1969 with a bachelor's degree in history and began a short-lived teaching career. He moved into sales before forming National Collection Office (NCO), which has gone from sixty clients to 80,000, from $70,000 in revenues to more than $700 million, and employs more than 10,000. As a motivational speaker, Chuck shares the useful tips and experienced wisdom he has gathered over his career. Visit www.chuckpiola.com.*

In His Hands

My husband, Mark, held my hand. A cold November chill hung in the air as we walked out the doors of the school, across the parking lot, and into the car without a word. We both knew in our hearts that this was the hardest thing we had ever done. As we pulled away from the school and onto the highway for the eighty-mile drive home, a knife was piercing my heart, and I could not stop the tears. Together we began to pray a prayer we've prayed so often:

Take, Lord, receive all my liberty,
My memory, my understanding,
And my entire will,
All that I have and possess.
You have given all to me,
To you, O Lord, I return it.
All is yours; dispose of it wholly according to your will.
Give me only your love and your grace,
For this is enough for me.

The school faded in the distance, but the memory of what had just happened did not. The scene played over and over in my mind. I saw my ten-year-old son, Patrick, pulling on my hand, wanting to leave with us. I saw the confusion in Patrick's eyes and the pain in Mark's. "Patrick, Mommy and Daddy have to go, but we will be back in a few days. The people here will take care of you." I tried to reassure him. "You will have fun with the other kids." As usual, he showed no sign that he understood a word. Patrick is a beautiful child with autism. Because he is unable to talk and has no functional form of communication, I search for answers in his big, dark eyes. All I saw that day was pleading. "Please take me with you. I don't want to stay here." Only by the grace of God was I able to pull away, leaving him in tears.

That night I couldn't sleep. I was so worried. "What if he is
cold or hungry?" I wondered. "What if he gets hurt, and he has
no one to hug him?" Through the tears, I prayed as never before,
asking God to send His angels to watch over him, and to protect
him. My heart was filled with so much love for my little son.
There was so much I wanted to tell him, and yet I didn't know
how. I asked God to help me find a way to make it through, and
before I knew it, I was writing a letter to Patrick. It was a letter I
knew he most likely would never read, but I wrote it nonetheless.
As the words left me and found their way onto the paper, the
burden on my heart began to lighten. I felt that God was telling
me, "I will tell Patrick what you write. He will know."

In my letter that first night, I wanted to let Patrick know how
much we loved him and that we wanted him home. I wanted him
to know that the reason he couldn't live at home right now was
because he needed help to find a way to communicate without
hitting. Patrick had become so strong that with one swing of his
arm he could send a two-year-old flying across the room. Usually
he showed no sign that he understood what he had done.

Mark and I felt very strongly that no matter what Patrick
needed, we always would take care of him and he would live in
our home with his three brothers and five sisters. God had shown
us, however, that we couldn't do it alone, and we had learned to
accept others' help, knowing it had come from Him. Until this
time, though, sending him to a residential school was not even
a possibility. When someone mentioned it to us once, we were
offended that they thought we would ever consider such a thing.
Now, here we were. We saw no alternative. Patrick would only
get bigger and stronger with time, and he needed more help than
we could give him.

I continued writing letters, and they gave me great comfort.
Still, there was a void. Even with a house full of children, my
arms ached to hold Patrick. I longed to take care of him. The
simple tasks that can seem like such a burden—washing his

clothes, fixing his meals, and cleaning up after him—became sweet treasures for which I longed.

One day, while folding laundry, I came across a shirt that Patrick used to wear. Mark had found it covered in mud by the creek in our back yard. As I folded the shirt, I remembered a day when Patrick was about eight. He had made so many messes that by the time I had cleaned up everything I had gone through an entire stack of towels I had just washed. In fact, it was the only laundry I had finished that day. God used Patrick and his ability to make major messes to teach me a valuable lesson. He taught me that there is only one reason to do laundry, and that is out of love for Him and not just to get it done. If I washed it for Him once, I can wash it again.

I had just told this story a few days before in a talk I was giving to a group of women. Often, after speaking at an event, people would tell me that it was the stories about Patrick that helped them. As I held his little blue shirt in my hand, the Lord spoke clearly to my heart, "Write the stories down." To many people this may not seem like much, but to me it was huge. I had always struggled with writing. I hadn't typed since college. "How could you actually want me to write all the stories?" I asked, almost pleading. The letters were one thing, but now the stories. I tried to reason that I didn't have time for such things, and I thought that maybe it was just a passing crazy idea that had jumped into my head.

Soon, the stories started to play in my head just like watching a movie. Before long, I started writing the stories. I wrote about how God had blessed our life with Patrick and the miracles that God had worked using my precious little son. I didn't know why I was writing. I just knew that I had to write.

One day while writing, the words "precious treasure" came to mind. *Yes*, I thought. *Patrick is our precious treasure.* I closed my eyes in prayer, and I saw my dresser, covered in precious family heirlooms, with a picture of Patrick in the center. "Is this what you want?" I asked God. I could not get the words or the picture out of my head. In my heart I knew this was indeed what He wanted.

I told Mark that I was going to put the stories together into a book. "Why don't you put the letters and the stories together?" He asked. "They go together very well."

"I'll keep the book for Patrick." I said. "Maybe someday he will be able to read. I want it to be here for him."

It wasn't long before friends and family started to read it and encourage us to seek publication. With the help of dear friends and the amazing grace of God, *Precious Treasure, the Story of Patrick*, was published and began to make its way across the United States and into many other countries. Soon letters began to come to me. They were letters from people who were helped by stories of a little boy who can't talk.

God allowed our son to be away from us so that He could use Patrick to bring others closer to Him. A man in his fifties, who had never been married and had no children, said it helped him deal with something he had been struggling with for fifteen years. A young girl going through chemotherapy wrote a beautiful note of how much it helped her make it through her treatments. A young mother told me that when she went for a routine prenatal ultrasound, the technician said something was wrong and went to get the doctor. The mother said, "I had just finished reading Patrick's book, and I know that God used it to give me comfort. I was at peace when the doctor told me what was happening with my baby girl."

One day, Mark was in a drugstore, and the pharmacist whom he barely knew said, "I just have to tell you what happened to me." She told of how she had foot surgery, the kind in which the doctor goes in and scrapes the bone. After the surgery she was in terrible pain. Despite all her knowledge of medications, she and the doctors could not get her pain under control. One night when she couldn't sleep because the pain was so intense, she picked up a package someone had sent. When she opened it, there was Patrick's book with a note, "I hope this helps you through a difficult night." She read the book straight through. She told Mark, "Not only did I completely forget about the pain while I was reading, but God used Patrick's story to help me put my whole life in perspective."

My dear Patrick is still away from me, and I continue to write him letters and to tell his stories. Patrick has been back home for short periods of time, but he continues to grow bigger and stronger and needs more help than we can give him. Through it all, God's grace has given us great strength to continually trust in His awesome plan. When Patrick was born, we gave our beautiful baby boy back to God. We placed him in the Father's hands. No matter how great the pain, no matter what happens, He will not let go. Our precious treasure is safe, of this we can be sure.

– Elizabeth Matthews

Elizabeth Matthews has been married for more than twenty-two years to her husband, Mark. The Matthews are the founders of Chelsea Shire Communications, a speaking and publishing apostolate dedicated to helping others live their Faith in simple yet extraordinary ways through God's abundant grace. She is the mother of twelve children. Elizabeth is the author of Precious Treasure *and co-author (with Mark) of* A Place for Me. *Recently, Elizabeth has been a contributing author to several books in the* Amazing Grace *series. Through her stories, she seeks to help others see God's blessings in all suffering and trials. Elizabeth has appeared on national radio and television, including EWTN's* Life on the Rock, The Abundant Life, *and* Bookmark. *She is a retired registered nurse and a frequent speaker on family, education, autism, and homeschooling issues.*

Triple Blessing

My husband, Dave, and I had lost five close relatives, including his mother, to death during the previous eighteen months. Losing so many loved ones quickly changed our view of life in a way that will reverberate into eternity. We went from thinking four children was our limit to making medical history with the birth of our identical triplets.

The odds of conceiving triplets naturally are just one in 8,100, and only six percent of those will be identical. And the odds of identical triplets surviving to birth with only one placenta were ... well, there were no odds. My doctor could find no record of it in the medical history books. Although I sometimes felt like a big experiment, I knew that God was behind it all. God, and my mother-in-law, who must have been whispering in His ear after her death from cancer.

With each of my four pregnancies, she would bless me and then recall tenderly how she had once been pregnant with triplets but lost them at eight weeks. "I would have loved to have triplets," she would add.

Dave had a paper delivery route and was a postman, and I was a private contractor with a crime lab. Between work and our kids—J.J., eighteen; Molly, seventeen; Elaine, eleven; and David, nine—our life was full. Neither Dave nor I felt we should have more children. But saying good-bye to so many loved ones helped us realize that there was nothing in this world more valuable than life. Dave and I both began to desire adding to our family. Our own children had brought us so much joy.

In February of 2004, we both hovered over the home pregnancy kit waiting for the results. "I'm pregnant!" I cried when a pink line emerged. We hugged and kissed, more excited than we had ever been before. I felt so privileged to be able to have another baby. Our children were excited, too. It had been a long time since we'd had a little one in diapers.

As a four-time mom, I expected this pregnancy to be routine, but from the start, it was different. My appetite became ravenous. I never liked milk, but suddenly I craved cereal and milk around the clock. In six weeks I had gained twenty pounds. Then, when morning sickness kicked in, I could no longer hold any food down. I also felt movement around my stomach and pain in my pelvic area. *Could it be an ectopic pregnancy?* Dave insisted on taking me to the doctors on March 31.

Dr. Dwayne Record sent us for a sonogram. I held Dave's hand while he stood at my side. Together, we looked at the monitor, fearful of what we might see. "There's one baby," the technician announced. Dave squeezed my hand as relief washed over us. "There are two babies," she continued.

"Oh, my goodness," I exclaimed. Dave and I laughed. I had wanted twins my whole life, and only days earlier Dave had joked with his co-workers that he was wishing a multiple birth on me.

"It gets better," the technician announced. "There's another one."

Dave and I were ecstatic. Triplets! We both immediately thought of his mom and the triplets she had lost at eight weeks. Moments earlier the doctor had told me I measured at eight weeks.

"But wait," the technician continued. "It gets even better. They are all identical." Dave and I looked at each other and cried tears of joy. I could not remember ever seeing Dave look so happy.

Then the doctor came in and looked at the screen. "There is a problem," he said solemnly. "There are three babies but only one placenta. This is bad news for both you and the babies. Even identical twins usually have their own placenta," he explained.

Our soaring spirits crash-landed as we learned that the odds for the survival of all three was not good. It would be difficult for them all to get enough nutrition from a shared placenta. Our tears had not stopped, but now they were of grief.

Dr. Record explained that he had once delivered triplets many years earlier and that he would do everything in his power to get us all through this, including praying for us. "God will look over you," he said.

We did not know how we would mange financially or emotionally, but we never doubted who was in charge. All we could do now was follow doctor's orders and pray to God to keep our babies alive if it was His will. Our small community rallied around us in many ways. My children's elementary school principal, Sister Helen Herman, had the whole school praying for us every morning. And not a day went by that Dave's postal customers were not asking about me and the babies.

At ten weeks, it was time for another sonogram. It was crucial that there be a thin membrane layer between each baby at this time if they were to continue to survive. We held our breath as the doctor examined the monitor. "Sure enough, there it is," he announced. At twenty weeks, we learned that babies A, B, and C were boys. But then, there was bad news. Two of the boys had cysts on their brains. This could mean serious mental or physical problems, although a detailed examination of the screen revealed no other abnormalities. We would just need to wait. "It's in your hands, God," I kept praying. "Please take care of my babies."

I could no longer work, and just getting out of bed had become a major task. At times, I feared for my health, the babies, and our finances. We did not even have insurance that covered the babies at that point. All the while, Dave kept telling me not to worry, that God was in charge. He was right. Somehow, we kept making it through another day. To my great relief, we learned that the triplets would be covered by Medicaid. And in spite of contractions at twenty-eight weeks, I was able to hang on until 34 weeks, which greatly improved the babies' odds.

When my contractions increased and my health became threatened, a C-section was quickly scheduled. On October 4, 2004, Anthony was lifted out first, weighing in at four pounds, one ounce. Chandler and Luke-Richard came out together, hugging each other and weighing three pounds, seven ounces, and four pounds, four ounces, respectively.

Gazing upon my triplets in the neonatal nursery for the first time, a wave of awe washed over me. All three were breathing on their own. Those three little lives came from Dave and me. They were God's little miracles. In just two weeks, the babies were healthy enough to bring home.

Our family will never be the same and we thank God for that. Although the boys all look alike, each has his own personality. Anthony is outgoing, Chandler is Mr. Personality, and Luke-Richard takes everything in stride. Although the boys have slight cerebral palsy, a condition common for premature babies, they all walked on their own between eighteen and twenty-three months. Their speech is slow, but all three are healthy and happy, and with continued physical and speech therapy, they are expected to do very well.

Our three boys have changed us forever. I feel so blessed. If I could hug God right now, I would hug Him and thank Him a hundred times over. My other children have grown in compassion and maturity. Our house has gotten smaller, but my kids would choose their little brothers over anything money can buy. They hold them, help care for them, and love them completely. Every step with the triplets has been a step closer to God for our family.

— Melody LaFountain

Melody LaFountain lives in New York state. She enjoys scrapbooking, coupon clipping, photography, drawing, painting, and teaching her triplets sign language. Melody was a travel agent for four years, but she now just likes to help family and friends plan their vacations.

Chapter 7

Life Is Precious

Melissa

Melissa was certainly not like the other children in the station wagon that picked up disabled kids from all over Oahu, Hawai'i, to take us to our respective schools. Today, her condition would be referred to as PVS, or "persistent vegetative state." There are degrees of disability, and the prejudice between these degrees can be sharper among us than they are noted among "normal people." The struggle to be considered as "normal" as possible can be a vicious, even cruel, yoke.

"I can play catch," a nine-year-old boy with hemophilia said, risking the easy breakage of his bones and bleeding which may be hard to stop to feel, just for a while, like an ordinary kid.

"I can roller skate faster than my sister!" said Dawn, who had practiced for months, and counted the bruises as nothing just so long as her total blindness wouldn't stop her from roller skating not only well *but faster* than her sister.

But Melissa did none of these things. She was on the "bottom" of the disability pyramid. Those who are thought to be, on the bottom are the little ones whom people let technology weed out by saying: "Isn't it wonderful we can perform tests now in the mother's uterus that reveal disabilities so it can be terminated?"

Very early in our lives, we know we must fight to be considered people. Unless we have parents and siblings and others around us who will help in our just fight to be considered human beings, we face a lonely struggle that is difficult beyond words to express.

But someone loved Melissa. Every day, her mother lovingly put her into the cab and kissed her good-bye. Melissa sat next to me day after day. She never said a word or reacted in any way to anything that happened around her.

We were picked up in the morning and driven to our different schools. I went to the school for "the deaf and the blind" — not "for deaf children" or "for blind children."

But Melissa went to a school where very little could be done for the children. Their disability seemed too great. Playing with colored balls, watching for reactions to see if things might be going on in those poor brains, and trying to stimulate any response were great steps forward.

I am ashamed to tell you this, but many time I said: "I'm not one of them! I can count and talk and sing and do lots of things Melissa can't do!" What I was really saying was, "I am not as disabled as Melissa, so I am more of a person than she is."

At the root of all this was fear. What if I couldn't be "normal," no matter how hard I tried? What if other people would not want my love because I am disabled? Other disabilities would develop as I got older. By then, I had the time and the love to realize that disability has nothing to do with being a full human being.

Melissa and the younger children and I sat in the front part of the station wagon. In back sat older kids, mostly deaf children. They had fun playing games with us younger ones, especially taunting and hurting the blind children, since, of course, we did not know who had hurt us. I know our kindly driver, Mr. Mayo, felt badly about all this, but it was hard for him to drive and attend to the craziness going on behind him at the same time.

One afternoon, one of the deaf children took a large wad of gum and smeared it all through my hair. This was followed by very hard hair pulling. I screamed with the pain. Mr. Mayo had not seen who had done it, and the laughter of the gang behind me frightened me. I began to cry hard, shaking and trembling.

Suddenly, two little arms were around me. A little hand touched my cheek. The little hand stroked my hair and cheek, and the little child who sat next to me day after day, nothing more than a "vegetable" to those pseudo-professionals, was rocking me in her arms. It was Melissa. I was so amazed that I stopped crying. This went on for about three minutes, and then, gently and tenderly, she touched my hair and cheek again, and went back into her own little world. I think the kids behind us were also amazed, because there was silence back there, too.

When I had pulled myself together, I gently put my arms around her, too, and we stayed like that for a long time. Every morning and afternoon that followed during the time we were together, we put our arms around each other again for a little while. After this, all disabled people became my people, and the hierarchy of disability existed for me no longer.

Melissa taught me that all people, especially the most disabled people, will always be my people. Quality-of-life criteria is nothing more than an evil way to justify killing unwanted people. I learned that if only one person is denied his or her humanity, none of us are safe, and none of us are "human."

– Patricia M. Devlin

Patricia Margaret Devlin was born in Hawai'i in 1953, before it was understood that varying levels of oxygen could destroy retina tissue and cause blindness. She was one of the many infants of this time who became blind as a result. Despite serious health problems, she worked, went to school, and almost got her doctorate, and raised her twin daughters alone. She is fighting her second bout with cancer, and through God's grace finds purpose in offering her chronic pain for others.

Survival of the Human Spirit

When I first saw him, words such as "despair," "gloom," "misery," and "despondency" came quickly to mind. He seemed sad and pitiful—a shadow of a man victimized by a system completely beyond his control.

It was during the summer of 2006 that I spent a week in Taxco, Mexico, a quaint mountain village abounding in temperate beauty while gracefully lacking in tourists. It is a place where I enjoyed practicing my limited Spanish on people with even more limited English.

Taxco's parish church is Santa Prisca. Its twin bell towers overlook the picturesque city square. Tucked off in one of the squares corners, and perhaps the only part of the square not appearing on postcards, there is an OXXO shop—Mexico's equivalent of 7-Eleven. During my time in Taxco, part of my morning ritual was stopping off at this shop to stock up on filtered water for the day, replace waning camera batteries, and buy sandwiches that left my stomach feeling so sour that I made empty promises to never purchase them again.

It was on these pleasant summer morning excursions to the OXXO that I encountered an old man who sat in front of the shop with a tin in front of him. It was aptly placed for people exiting the store to unburden themselves of leftover pesos. Unlike the many eager beggars I have encountered during past excursions to Central America, this one had his head always bowed as if slumbering. I got the impression he was completely apathetic to the world around him—as if any donations to his little tin cup would only allow him to sustain his misery longer. For six mornings, when I left the OXXO I dropped a few pesos into his tin and heard the resulting clink—the tune of a good deed.

On those first six mornings, I don't recall the man ever looking up to see who it was dropping coins barely worth the metal composing them into his dish. On Sunday, my last day in

Taxco, my purchases had been to the correct peso, leaving me coinless. I rested that day from making the man's tin clink.

As I walked out of the door, ready to hop into a van bound for Mexico City, I gazed at the lovely city square for the last time, thinking of how I would miss it. My thoughts were interrupted by a voice that called out to me. I turned and, to my surprise, saw the old man looking up, beckoning me toward him. I reached into my pockets searching for some loose pesos. I assumed money could be the only reason he summoned me.

I squatted down next to the man, and greeted him with a warm *hola*. It was then that I saw for the first time what his bowed head and gray hat hid beneath. Looking up at me were the deepest brown eyes and the truest smile that I have ever seen. He warmly shook my hand and asked me what country I was from. My Caucasian features pegged me an obvious outsider. I told him I was a college student from the United States, to which he jovially nodded his smiling head. He asked me how long I was going to stay in Taxco, where I was going later, and other such small talk. I barely listened to his questions. I was too taken aback at the deep joy that I found in this man. It simply did not fit. The American dream from the world I came from did not allow for such happiness in the face of nothingness.

His happiness both intrigued and puzzled me. Because of my limited Spanish, I was not able to ask anything more compelling than a simple, "Why are you so happy? (*Por que estas tan alegre?*) His reply left an imprint on my heart.

The man smiled and looked deeply into my eyes. He was my elder and seemed patiently amused that I needed to ask about something he must have thought obvious. He slowly and eloquently replied, "*Porque el mundo es un lugar magnifico*" (Because the world is a magnificent place). Then he shook my hand and wished me happy travels. I walked away, looking back at the man several times. The city square seemed different from when I had entered it fifteen minutes earlier.

Yes, the world *can* be a magnificent place. But for the beggar on the street? For an old man who spends his days hoping people will throw a few pesos into a can so that he can eat? Is the world a magnificent place for the man I pitied? For that old man who sat outside the OXXO with a tin can, it was. In him I found a smile where I suspected a scowl. I saw hopeful eyes where I thought despair resided. Most importantly, I found pure happiness survived where it seemed impossible.

– Luke Armstrong

Luke Armstrong is a co-editor of Amazing Grace for Survivors. *His biography appears at the end of the book.*

A Former Altar Boy on Death Row

Ron Keine refused to become one of those people who find religion in prison on the way to death row. *No, he decided, repenting is for the ones who are here for a reason. I have done nothing wrong.*

Ron felt the justice system was a joke. "Justice was only a word that the court system was using to put four innocent men, myself among them, to death in New Mexico for a murder we did not commit," he said

As the days drew closer to his publicly administered death, his faith in God withered. "You did this to me, God," Ron cried out. "I'm not going to get on my knees and beg, because I don't want your help! I am an innocent man!"

Not long before the date of the execution, the men decided: *They may take everything from us, but it's we who will take our own lives.* They planned to do themselves in as a way to hold onto a small shred of the freedom that unjust men had ripped away from them. But as the reality of such a choice sank in, something stopped Ron. *Wait, hold on*, he realized. *If I do that, I'll go to hell.* He knew there was something even worse than death row.

Ron looked at his life and could not believe how it had turned out. What would the Ron of years before, the altar boy from Detroit, have said if he could envision sitting in a prison cell, days away from an execution by the state of Arizona? After high school, Ron rebelled and joined one of Detroit's motorcycle clubs. His best friend, Doc, convinced him to ride to California. They were young, had bikes, and wanted a free-spirited life. On February 14, 1972, the day after Ron got his mechanic certification, Doc and he rode the cold Northern Route all the way to California. They arrived in California and joined the "baddest" motorcycle gang out there.

After a couple years riding in California, Doc and Ron and three of their club brothers decided to return to Detroit for a visit.

Since it was winter, they all piled into a van. As the group drove, they saw two hippie hitchhikers and decided to give them a lift. The hippies looked a little intimidated upon seeing the van full of five bikers, but they were greeted with beers and welcomed. Then one of the hippies was caught shoving beers into his knapsack. It resulted in their getting put out on the road, one with a black eye.

A couple hours after the hippies were dishonorably discharged, six police squad cars pulled over the van and arrested all five of them. The hippies had used a pay phone to alert the police to the van. The five of them were charged with armed robbery of a party store on Route 40. It went to trial but was dismissed when the judge realized that the party store that they allegedly had robbed had burned down two years earlier.

When the judge threw out the trial, the detainees expected to be released. Instead, after a couple weeks, two detectives from Albuquerque, New Mexico, extradited them to their state. Suddenly, what seemed like an inconvenient incident turned into the five men being charged by the state prosecutor with murder in the first degree. In the mountains outside of Albuquerque, the body of a New Mexican college student had been found. Though these men had not even been in the area, it did not matter to the prosecution. The whole ordeal was a sham. Even before the trial began, the five had moved from the jail to death row and were told: "Get used to it, because that's where you're going to end up."

To their utter disbelief and complete horror, the verdict at the trial was guilty and the sentence was death. Still, Ron would not turn to God: "I would not pray, because any God who would let an innocent man die like this was not one I wanted to talk to."

When Ron was weeks away from his death, a South Carolina drifter, the real murderer, read about the trial in a paper. He walked into a Southern Baptist church, where he had a conversion, and then went to New Mexico and confessed. Amazingly, the prosecutor refused to hear the confession, stating that those responsible were already behind bars. The imprisoned men had been back to court five times, but motioning for a new trial was always shot down.

Then, one of the men on death row had a girlfriend back in Michigan who alerted a court reporter from the *Detroit News* that her boyfriend, also from Michigan, was about to be executed in the state of Arizona. As the reporter investigated and perused through files on the case, he inquired as to why so many of the documents were missing. That night, two deputies knocked on his motel door and told him to get the hell out of town unless he wanted to end up on death row, too. This reporter had covered the court beat for twenty-two years. After this incident, he called his boss, who sent two more reporters to Arizona.

This put the wheels in motion. Judge Vernon Payne ordered a retrial. The holes in the case were easily revealed. For example, the man, who had testified as the pathologist for the murder victim, was found to have been paid $50,000 for his false testimony. The woman whose testimony had sent the men to death row, was ready to tell the truth—something she had always wanted to do but had been blackmailed by the prosecutors. The reporter had tracked her down in Minnesota. Once she was assured that there would be no retaliation against her, she was only too happy to testify. The woman revealed that she had been tutored in what to say and how to say it. In the end, a week before the men's execution date, the original indictments were dismissed in a retrial. The murder weapon was eventually traced to the real killer, who confessed to the crime.

"After the verdict, one of the guards was trying to handcuff me again," Ron recalls. So he indignantly asked the guard: "Are you arresting me for something?"

"We need to sign you out," he said.

"I did not sign to get in, and I'm not signing to get out," Ron stated. "Your honor, would you tell this man I'm free?"

"I need to take these men back to process them for release," the guard said.

Looking at the men, the judge asked: "Do any of you want to go back?"

They all shook their heads and walked out into sweet freedom after twenty-two months on death row.

Convicts on parole—who were guilty of the crimes they had served time for—have programs to help them find jobs and places to live. These men were given nothing. Their lawyer arranged for some clothing, and Ron hitched a ride back to Michigan with the reporter from the *Detroit News*. The other three returned to California to the biker gang. Within a few years, two of them were killed in gang violence and the third, Doc, had committed suicide.

Ron explains that his own family was pretty dysfunctional. He was estranged from them, leaving him without strong support. He found friends to stay with and sometimes lived on the streets. "I did what I could to survive, doing odd jobs and eventually working as a plumber," he explains. "Initially, the rage I carried against those who had hurt me boiled up within me. I could not sleep at night and was still angry with God. But eventually, I spoke with a nun who changed everything. 'It's okay that you feel angry with God,' she told me. 'But you need to give everything over to Him.'"

Ron says he did not understand what she was saying. "This is more than you can handle," she explained. "Tell God of your anger and hurt, and tell Him you are giving everything over to Him. He will carry this burden for you. But there is one more thing you must do," she added. "You must forgive those who have hurt you."

Ron did not see how he could possibly forgive, but this nun told him: "You will just let them continue to hurt you if you let the anger eat away at you."

Ron went home that night, and for the first time in a long time, he spoke with God. "I told him 'It's all yours, I can't take it anymore.' Then, I told Him I was worn out by the anger and sleepless nights. I asked Him to help me to do the seemingly impossible: to forgive those who had committed such evil against me. 'I don't know why you did this to me,' I prayed. 'Maybe it was to stop me from the life I was living, but this hate thing is part of what I got. Help me to stop it.'"

By the next day, Ron was a different person. He says it was like a boulder that had been pinning him down was lifted off his heart. He could finally sleep again. For about a week he struggled with forgiveness, but then it came, slowly and easily. It had once infuriated him that God allowed him to go to prison for something he did not do, but Ron says he now believes that if all that had not happened to him, he would either have been killed or have killed someone himself, given the life he lived as part of the biker gang. Today, over thirty years after his imprisonment on death row, Ron says he has a greater purpose for having lived through such a nightmare.

Ron travels around the country speaking against the death penalty as part of an organization called Witness to Innocence. He says he feels he can make a difference in the lives of others who are so often forgotten by society. "It's easy to lose faith when things seem awful, but now I know that sometimes it's these terrible struggles that God uses to build us into the people He needs us to be," he says. When Ron speaks at schools and universities, he urges people to vote for politicians who oppose the death penalty. "I know that I am doing God's work to respect the life of every human being—work that I would not be doing if I had not been an innocent man ten days away from execution," he says.

Ron explains that he speaks out for everyone on death row, not just the innocent. "God is the author of all life. When people tell me the Bible says: 'An eye for an eye, a tooth for a tooth,' I tell them that statement was a tribal law of limitation to get war-like men to tone it down and not try to take out the whole clan in retribution. God did not kill Abel or Moses after they killed people. There were no prisons back then, so the laws were harsh.

In the New Testament, Jesus came to clarify things and taught forgiveness and love."

Ron explains further: "I do this now for my three brothers who aren't here anymore and I do it for those who are locked away and forgotten. Knowing that I'm working for God makes me feel richer than anything else this world could offer."

– Luke Armstrong

Luke Armstrong is a co-editor of Amazing Grace for Survivors. *His biography appears at the end of the book.*

Don't Jump

My wife woke up and saw me standing above her, next to the bed. I was dressed but not in work clothes. "Trish, there is something wrong with me. I tried to kill myself. I was driving around. I was going to drown myself."

Trish got me to lie down, and she covered me with a blanket. Then, she called my office and left a message for my boss that I would not be in for the rest of the week. Things were seriously wrong. She got Kristen, age twelve, and Ryan, ten, the youngest of our four kids still at home, off to school then called my doctor.

"This is Patricia Gallagher," she explained. "I am John Gallagher's wife. He has been in to see you a few times. Doctor, he needs to go somewhere to have a rest." She continued: "He has been driving around for an hour this morning. Doctor, something is wrong. Where can I take him?" Trish made arrangements to take me to Warminster Hospital, where there was a psychiatric unit. It was a beautiful day, but as usual, my mood was totally flat.

As we drove on, I said plainly, "I'm going to die."

"No, John, you are just stressed," Trish insisted. "You need a vacation."

As we parked in the hospital parking lot, I said, "I'm going to die. I took carbon monoxide." I confessed that when I was driving around at 6:00 a.m., I pulled the car over and breathed the exhaust for ten minutes. I did not want to talk about it any more than that.

As a man in this world of ours, I am expected to hold a job, make enough money to pay my bills, provide for my four children, and be there for my wife. But sometimes in the hustle and bustle of everyday life all the tasks and responsibilities build up into an overwhelming stress. That's what happened to me nine years ago. On the outside, everything looked great. I had an MBA, a job as a financial analyst, a wife, and four children. But on the inside, everything began falling apart. My company was cutting back, and I feared being unable to provide for my family. Life began to overwhelm me.

During this time, one night, a darkness stirred inside me. I awoke and felt my brain racing in a way I had never experienced. I prayed to God for this scary feeling to leave, but it did not. I got up, walked downstairs, and turned the TV on. My head throbbed and my heart raced. *Could this be an anxiety attack?* I wondered. *Or a heart attack?* I began pacing up and down the house, holding my agonizing head and wondering what it could be. The noise of my footsteps awoke Trish.

"What are you doing?" she asked, sleepily.

"I don't know," I responded. The pain in my head writhed as I spoke. "I think I'm having some sort of chemical imbalance in my brain."

She called the doctor, who listened to my symptoms. He thought I was having some sort of anxiety attack and suggested that I lie down and try to relax, but this did not help.

After a restless night, I still had the pressing headache from the night before. Though I didn't feel like I could do anything, I went to work. It was a stressful job from which I got little joy.

At work, I couldn't concentrate on anything. Everything faded into nothingness and seemed unreal compared to the ever-present, searing pain splitting my head in two. Though my coworkers noticed I was not myself, they had no idea just how disoriented I felt.

The next day, I knew it was not likely to be something that would just go away. I went to our family doctor. He listened patiently and prescribed a drug for anxiety. But he had misdiagnosed me, so the drug did not help.

I went back to see him. "It's not going away," I reported.

"Well, it will take about three weeks for the medicine to work. Just give it time," was his answer.

What I know now but did not know then, was that a family

doctor is ill equipped to deal with the sort of chemical imbalance that was going on inside of me. I needed to see a psychiatrist.

My wife tried to be supportive, but she felt as helpless as I did. We both trusted the medication to work, but as time dragged on, the unbearable feeling in my head persisted. I would go to the doctor filled with hope, and then go with my wife to a healing Mass, where I pleaded, *please, God, let this be it;* but I always returned home still unable to sleep and without relief from the headache. As time went on, my situation only worsened. In addition to the pain, anxiety surged as heart palpitations took my breath away. Sleepless nights became the norm, and eating became a chore. I simply had no appetite. I lost sixty pounds and wore two sets of clothing to hide how thin I had become. Feelings were absent. I could not concentrate and felt powerless. My wife and kids were supportive and loving, but everyone was getting frustrated.

I tried everything I could think of to put an end to the darkness. From a multitude of doctors, to healing Masses and prayers. Nothing seemed to help. I felt betrayed by God.

Yet, the demands to function in my life did not abate. But I reached the point where I could not go on. I was a shadow of my former self. Suffering was one thing, but the feeling of abandonment and loneliness was unbearable.

Yes I had tried to kill myself by breathing in exhaust fumes, but I had suddenly stopped when I realized my link with God, though thin and worn, was not completely worn away. He still had a hold on me. I knew my life was only mine to live, not to take.

At the hospital, my blood pressure was still very high, and so they took me to the cardiology department in an attempt to lower my blood pressure before tackling the other problems. My wife stood patiently by the hospital bed. She showed me pictures of our kids. The pictures were meant to cultivate some feelings of happiness in me. Instead, I felt all the more desperate, convinced that the best was all behind me now. Then, Trish left the room to phone the children.

Alone in my room, I thought that the best of life was now in the past and could only haunt me. My twisted thinking led me to imagine that the doctors would commit me to an insane asylum. Near my bed, a pleasant breeze drifted in from the window, which was ajar. I looked at the window as an end to my suffering. I arose from my bed and approached the window. The raw throbbing in my head had dulled my thought process so I acted without much thought beyond a drive to escape. I looked down the three stories. *I can do it*, I thought. *I will do it.* I jumped, relieved that the pain would finally go away. It did not.

I landed on my legs, and then crumpled. Rage exploded inside me. *I'm still alive,* I cried. *I could not even kill myself.* I lay on the asphalt bleeding and cursing my survival. Landing on my legs had saved my life, but they were now crushed and broken. The police and ambulance arrived in minutes.

"Cut his jeans off!" one of the paramedics yelled as they slid me onto a stretcher. Voices shouting commands seemed far away until they faded into nothingness. I fell into unconsciousness.

A doctor awakened me. "Turn your neck," he said, worried that it could be broken. It was not broken, but I had completely crushed both legs and had head and arm abrasions. The doctors told my wife that I still had a very good chance of dying. There were bone chips in my blood stream that had caused a blood infection that could have succeeded where I had failed—ending my life.

My wife relayed this message to me. Her patience through it all was disarming. "I want you to know that I love you, the kids love you, we just want you to get better, and whatever you need we will do for you." Every day she came in to reassure me. "Don't worry about work, don't worry about money, and don't worry about getting better. As soon as you start getting better you'll go home, and I'll take care of you."

The jump landed me a stay in the mental ward of the hospital with twenty-four-hour security. I was there for five weeks. I needed both physical and mental healing. A psychiatrist was assigned to me and we began work on my mind while an orthopedic surgeon worked on putting my legs back together.

After being released from the hospital, I still had to do physical therapy to help repair my battered body while I saw a therapist and went to cogitative therapy sessions to help repair my life. The antidepressants began to kick in, and I started to be able sleep again at nights while my headaches started to fade into a bad memory.

Though I was on the road to recovery, I was still very irritable and weak from losing nearly sixty pounds and being confined for a time to a wheelchair. Though my family was supportive, it became a lot for anyone to handle. One night my wife turned to me. "I can't do this anymore, John," she said. "I need to ask you to leave."

Trish had been going to the monastery of the Poor Clares every day for a visit to pray. She was also going to a family therapist, who said, "Trisha, by the look in your eyes and from all that you have told me, I am worried about you. Your children need at least one healthy parent. I think that you and John need to separate so that you can both work on things and heal separately. You can continue to see each other and plan a date once a week, but for now, it is too much."

I knew I had been miserable to live with, and Trish and I struggled to get along, but I did not want to be alone. However, it was clear that she had already made up her mind. "It will be better if you go your way. I'll try to heal, and get better. You go to therapy, and we'll heal separately."

We maintained our relationship, but it was more of a friendship than a marriage. I was still there regularly to be a father to my kids. We all got together every Sunday and holidays. I never stopped loving my family.

During this painful time for our family, something powerful was at work. While I was struggling with depression but before

I actually jumped, Trish had begun writing poems as a way of coping. She called upon a team of angels to help. The first poem was titled "A Team of Angels for the Overwhelmed." She paired each poem with a little trio of angels pin that she created from materials she purchased at a craft store. She began making them by the hundreds and passing them out for free. The three angels represented peace in our hearts, peace in our homes, and peace in the world. Over the next few years, the angels became her lifeline after the tragedy. Soon, people worldwide requested them by the thousands after a mention in *Family Circle* magazine.

And little by little, almost without even noticing, we did heal. Medication and cognitive therapy sessions slowly gave me back my life. I also took a less stressful job selling clothing. Trish asked me to come home after a five-year separation. The life I had thought was only a memory began to return. Healing is a long process, but certainly led by a team of angels, I began to heal, as did our family.

On February 2, 2006, the day that I returned to live with my family, a new chapter began for us. Trish scheduled a Retrouvaille weekend, which helps couples in troubled marriages improve their relationships. We found the tools to bring healing and continued with counseling. Then, there was something else that brought us closer; Trish wanted to take the angel pin project to a different level. Through our pain and healing had come a new idea. She wanted to travel nationwide with me to distribute thousands of angel pins to those in need of comfort.

Although Trish had started the team of angels pin project, it was going to continue with me at the helm of her new campaign. Over the first six years, she had survived on contributions and distributed 78,500 "Team of Angels" lapel pins with a prayer card explaining the project and encouraging people to keep passing the pin onto others also in need. She received 30,000 heartwarming letters and grim stories from a wide variety people from around the world: a prisoner on death row; a woman whose triplets were killed by a drunk driver; a child who had been abused; and a young girl who credited the pin with helping her find a kidney donor.

It became a ministry that we shared together. In the summer of 2006, I joined Trish and our son Ryan and a couple of his friends, traveling from Pennsylvania to Florida, then up to New England and out to Ohio. We took pins to people in need at hospitals, addiction centers, and even to the homeless in the streets. We traveled 7,000 miles in all in a rented gold van with a sign attached to the side panel reading: "Are you overwhelmed? Ask us for a free angel pin and then kindly pass it along."

Although the pins were initially all given away, in order to continue to afford this venture, Trish's project turned into a family business/ministry as a way to offer people a small token of encouragement. God's angels truly transformed our family's pain from healing into a ministry of encouragement to others. Reaching out to others who were suffering helped bring Trish and me closer together. I realized that the road to healing is like the road to Calvary. But it is a road that we do not need to walk alone because God will send us an army of angels to walk with us and guide us down right paths.

Then, on January 20, 2008, I discovered there was still another chapter left in all of this. I read a newspaper story about a high school student who had survived a nine-story jump. What struck me was that he was willing to speak out about his experience. It was then that I realized that sharing my story could help others. And that is just what is happening. Now that I have begun speaking out, people come forward to thank me. Some are dealing with depression in their own families. Reaching out to others has helped our own family to heal. Instead of hiding, Trish and I are sharing the truth about the pain we went through. Our children too have told us they now understand.

I never would have chosen the path of pain I have walked. But now, I can see that by turning to God through it all, Trish and I have grown closer to Him and to each other. I am living proof that no matter how bad things get, there is always a road towards healing that is paved with angels.

— John Gallagher

John and Patricia Gallagher welcome speaking engagements to share their story of faith and hope. John is the author the book Don't Jump: A Father's Journey Through Depression. *They live in Pennsylvania with their four children, Robin, Katelyn, Kristen, and Ryan. Their family ministry, The Team of Angels Project, has touched over 100,000 people by providing a special angel pin attached to an inspirational poem. For more information, visit www. teamofangels.com.*

Steadfast Love

"Yes, I want to continue with the adoption of Patrick." Those words resonated throughout my soul as my husband, Tullio, firmly expressed them without a hint of doubt. Our Vietnamese adoption presented us with one major obstacle after the next. At times, for me, it made our pursuit of this particular child seem hopeless. I began to question if this was really meant to be. After all, if God wanted this to happen, it would, but it just was not happening. I had begun to question if perhaps we should begin looking elsewhere. Our adoption agency even offered us the option of selecting a different child or adopting from a different country. But Tullio was unmoved. His trust that our Lord wanted Patrick to be our son was certain.

We had already adopted three precious children from various countries. Francesco, from Mexico, was now four years old, and Analisa, from Guatemala, was three. Teresa, from India, was born the same year as Patrick, 1997, but unexpectedly she had arrived several months earlier. Since I had been to India on a mission trip and had worked with Mother Teresa, I had a special connection to that country. Having been to India, I expected I would go to Vietnam to get Patrick and visit his country, and then I would be back and ready to bring Teresa into our home. Instead, it turned out that Teresa came to us before Patrick while paperwork stalled his adoption. This whole situation turned my plans upside down.

The culprit for the delay was an obscure document that the United States Immigration and Naturalization Service demanded and the Vietnamese authorities refused to provide. The attempt to obtain this from across the ocean and through jungles and red tape was proving next to impossible. One-and-a-half years after we had begun the adoption processes, Teresa had been with us three months, but there was still no sign of getting Patrick.

Suddenly, after being told it would be at least several more months, we received a call from the agency: "Make travel arrangements as soon as possible, but realize there is no guarantee you will be coming back with Patrick." I did not want to leave our new baby, Teresa, and our plan to have Tullio come was impossible since it was in the middle of his busiest work season as a certified public accountant—tax season.

As the obstacles continued, my heart filled with despair. I began to feel that as each hurdle was overcome, another appeared in its place. The forces to prevent us from adopting Patrick seemed so strong that I began to wonder: *Perhaps our desire to adopt Patrick really wasn't God's will, but only our own.*

But in the midst of my doubt, Tullio's steadfast trust in the Lord quieted my fears. "This is my son, and I am going to do whatever it takes to get him," he stated. One afternoon, Tullio brought home a large framed picture of Mother Teresa looking down with a peaceful joy. As I gazed upon it, it seemed that maybe this saintly woman whom I felt such a connection with was looking down on a child—a child like Patrick. I felt her presence calm my fears.

Following Tullio's advice, I took some time alone in our modest home chapel and turned everything over to God. "Lord, I just want to hear you," I prayed. Suddenly, I felt assurance that Patrick, indeed, was under God's sovereignty.

The hurdles and complications were unrelenting. Everything from missing a flight due to severe weather to an airline bus getting stuck and luggage getting lost continued the seemingly endless saga. Still, my peace was not shaken. What should have taken only a couple weeks turned into a four-and-a-half-week odyssey. On my first Tuesday in Saigon, Patrick was placed in my arms. Looking into his angelic face and beautiful dark eyes, I measured an emotional distance between us by hardening my heart. I was allowed to take him to the hotel to stay with me, but I was reminded that I might not be taking him home. "I am excited to finally meet you," I told the little guy, who I was told connected with me instantly, "but I'm not falling in love." By Friday, only three days later, while sitting in our stark hotel room awaiting the negotiation of the document, I looked into Patrick's face and watched his expressions. Suddenly, I realized I was hopelessly in love. I knew I did not want to leave without him and trusted that I would take him home.

The Vietnamese officials did not share my confidence. I had been to Third World and Eastern countries many times, but this was one adventure I did not want. I had to make three trips back and forth to the remote region Patrick was from, traveling with an adoption liaison between the government officials and the orphanage. After my third return to Saigon, empty-handed, the adoption liaison called within a few days and informed me that it had been worked out that I could leave without the document. In the end, the final documentation was not provided until Tullio and I were able to finalize the adoption in the United States.

Our homecoming at 5:20 a.m. was a quiet one, when I finally placed our son into his daddy's waiting arms. Seeing Tullio's loving look at his new son filled me with appreciation that his strong, steadfast love was really what had brought our baby home. I felt so blessed and happy to be home again, surrounded by my beautiful children and husband. The long wait for Patrick had been worth every minute.

Within a couple weeks of my return, in April of 1998, I took Patrick to the pediatrician's office. He seemed very healthy, but I wanted to get him in for a well-baby check-up. Although, he was checked after he was born for hepatitis B, there is an incubation period before the body shows the markers. Consequently, he was rechecked for hepatitis B. I received the shattering news over the phone. Patrick had an active case of hepatitis B, likely contracted at birth. After consulting with numerous medical specialists and undergoing multiple tests, in the winter of 2001, I was told that there was nothing medical science could do to stop this dreadful form of the disease in a young child. It was expected to eventually take Patrick's life. After all we went through to get Patrick, we were going to lose him. Our supposedly healthy, bouncing, baby boy was just given a death sentence—an active and aggressive case of mutated hepatitis B.

Tullio was alarmed, but not shaken. It seemed we had only brought Patrick home to die. In spite of his outward healthy appearance, this blood-borne disease was destroying his liver. There was no treatment for him. On one level, life continued as normal. The kids ran around, played, laughed, cried … all the usual stuff. But on another level, nothing was the same. Each interaction and glance with our son underscored how much I loved him and mourned his diagnosis. *How much time would he have with us? How would we care for both him and the others as his health deteriorated?* He held our hearts in his embrace as I tried to accept the steady progress of his diagnosis. I just could not accept losing the son I had fought so hard to adopt. In church one day, I pleaded with God for Patrick's life. I looked up at the altar and suddenly, in my mind's eye, envisioned a coffin with him in it. It was too much to bear. I broke down sobbing. The mother of a good friend who was nearby, put her arms around me and cried with me.

We invoked the prayers of hundreds of people, including the Missionaries of Charity (from three different countries) to pray, especially asking for the intercessory prayers of Mother Teresa. I lamented to Tullio: "I don't think he will be cured." Tullio gently reassured me: "God will cure Patrick in His own time, even if it requires medication." Since we had been told there was no treatment available for Patrick, nothing short of a miracle could save him.

When I spoke with my former spiritual director, I told her how desperately we wanted Patrick to live. "You need to realize that God gave you Patrick to love and care for him, but he belongs to God," she counseled me. "Take him to the foot of the cross and give him back to Jesus. "

I took Patrick to the foot of the altar and told God, "He is yours. Do with him what you will. Whatever happens to this child, just let us give glory to you." I so desperately wanted our son to live, but I was finally ready to submit to God's will. I was filled with peace and stopped trying to emotionally fight it anymore.

Within a few weeks of completing the novena, Patrick's physician excitedly called us one day. He was corresponding with scientists in Hong Kong and had stumbled upon some surprising news. They were using a treatment involving a combination of four medicines that could possibly irradiate the hepatitis B to a point where it would become inactive. But again, red tape and delays dimmed our hope. Not all the drugs had approval for use in this country. Only one of the four medications, Epivir (Lamivudine) could be obtained, reducing Patrick's chances. Because of the nature of his hepatitis, the physician stated that it would be at least a year before we would know if the medication would help at all.

Amazingly, in only one month after the start of the medication, our physician called and enthusiastically reported that the viral DNA (the genetic material that indicates the presence and reproduction of the virus) had plunged from the 2,300 range to the range of two. This was so remarkable that the test had to be rechecked for accuracy. In less than one year the DNA was completely absent, and he was taken off medication.

Later tests revealed that Patrick's immune system now made the two types of antibodies needed to kill off the hepatitis B. He was completely cured, which is a rarity for hepatitis B. Also, Patrick's previous liver damage had also repaired itself.

I often reflect on the journey to adopt Patrick. Had it not been for Tullio's resolve, our son would have soon been deemed ineligible for adoption. Patrick would have spent the rest of his limited life in an impoverished orphanage where the opportunity to be cured of hepatitis B was non-existent. Instead, today, at the age of ten, he is a healthy, vibrant child. We fought hard for Patrick, twice. Both times, just as I thought we would lose him for sure, I gave him over to God. And both times, God blessed us abundantly and gave him back to us.

— Nancy Patin Falini

Nancy Patin Falini is a registered dietitian, consultant, author, and national lecturer specializing in celiac disease. She and her husband live in West Chester, Pennsylvania, with their four internationally adopted, homeschooled children.

Survival Day-by-Day

It's a nightly tradition. After evening prayers are said, dishes washed, and my three daughters and one son have drifted off into a quiet slumber, I walk into three-year-old Catherine's room as she peacefully rests. Like many fathers, I look at my beautiful daughter with a mixture of awe and gratitude, thanking God for such a precious gift. The sight of her chest rising and falling with her breath gives my wife, Becky, and me the ease to go to sleep ourselves.

Catherine, the youngest of our children, was born at home. In the first year of her life, she seemed remarkably healthy. At fourteen months, Catherine's health unexpectedly and drastically changed. She was irritable and run down, so initially we wondered if it was teething or a virus. Catherine began drinking water and urinating constantly. It got to the point that that we had to change her diaper and pajamas at least once during the night. We set up a doctor's appointment. Throughout the day of the appointment, I carried her around the house. She was hardly moving and could barely raise her head off my shoulder.

I stayed home with the other three children while my wife took her to the doctor's office. Upon their arrival in the doctor's office, the nurses took one look at her and immediately moved her to the front of the line. As my wife described the symptoms, the nurse took one of her used diapers and ran a glucose test on the urine. "You need to take her to the hospital immediately," she told Becky. "We think she has the onset of diabetes."

My wife called me from the doctor's office to tell me what had just transpired. As my wife described what they had told her, tears welled up in my eyes. I had worked in a camp for children with diabetes a few years earlier. I was familiar with the condition and knew what it meant for a fifteen-month-old baby to have it. My mind swirled, realizing how this would change everything as I quickly arranged for a neighbor to watch the other kids so I could meet Becky at the hospital.

We walked into the emergency room together with Catherine. Once again, Catherine was moved to the front of the line. After drawing her blood and starting an IV, they pointed out that she was having small seizures from her extremely high blood sugar. She spent the next two days in the intensive care unit while Becky and I took turns watching over her twenty-four hours a day. I called everyone I knew, asking them to please pray for our little girl. Catherine was put on every prayer chain we could think to contact.

We watched anxiously as her small face began to improve, and the little girl we loved so much began to return. On her third day in the hospital, one of the nurses brought in a little red wagon filled with stuffed animals and toys. We loaded her in and wheeled a much healthier looking Catherine into a room in the pediatric wing.

In the four days Catherine spent there, Becky and I became experts on the disease. We learned how to monitor her blood sugar levels. Our daughter would depend dearly on our using our knowledge with precision.

Diabetes is an extremely intense disease to deal with in a small child, because you cannot predict when and how much the child is going to eat. It requires constant vigilance of testing blood sugar to make sure it does not get too high or too low. There is no room for error. Too high and she could face long-term damage, such as kidney failure, amputations, loss of feeling, or loss of eyesight. Too low, and she could pass out, have a seizure or even go into a coma and die.

Medical conditions and dealing with them are part of our family's life now. Since the diagnosis of her condition, my other three children have been diagnosed with some sort of autoimmune diseases. As fathers, we all have fears for our children, both for the present and the future. For my daughter

Catherine, a very tangible fear is present on a daily basis. If I don't make sure she has eaten her food after an injection, then she could end up sick, at the very least, or even have a reaction that poses a significant threat to her life.

For her, the world is a very dangerous place. Things we take for granted, like sneaking an extra few cookies or skipping lunch, can seriously harm her. It is humbling to realize how little control we sometimes have over small things that carry great importance. My wife works in the nutritional supplement industry, and there are some in her industry who think that taking the right supplements can cure almost anything. With diabetes, there is nothing you can do to stop it. It leaves us with only one perspective; God is in control here. In the end, it is the same for all of us. We can do our best in whatever situation we are placed, but in the end, our life is beyond our control, so we best rest in the Lord.

So we pray for her condition often, and we pray that some day a cure will be found. And in the meantime, we trust that God does not do things without a reason. He gave us our wonderful daughter, and we know that, despite her condition, she is perfect in His eyes.

– Chris Cash

Chris Cash is the director of e-commerce for CatholicCompany.com, the most popular Catholic store on the Internet. He is also the host of CatholicSpotlight. com, an Internet radio show that features hot new books and other products in the catholic marketplace. His wife, Becky, is a very successful independent Shaklee distributor who specializes in helping moms earn an income working from home. Becky can be contacted at becky@getfed.com or 1-800-937-4615.

The Baby Who Would Not Die

In my hometown of Sighisoara, Romania, lives a woman named Magdalena. She, her husband, and their three children lived in a house with her husband's parents, as did her husband's brother and his family. The three families, six adults and four children, made for a very cramped household.

This was during the Communist regime of the dictator Nicolae Ceausescu, who ruled Romania from 1965 to 1989. Life was hard. It was necessary to stand in long lines to buy food, and sometimes there was none to buy.

When Magdalena became pregnant with her fourth child, a fierce verbal battle erupted in the extended family. The grandparents and other family members wanted the child to be aborted because there was not enough money coming in to feed and clothe the children they already had. Magdalena's mother-in-law said, "She has no skills to enable her to earn income; all she can do is have babies." Magdalena desperately wanted to keep the child, but finally, with deep sorrow, she relented to keep peace in the family.

Abortion was illegal in Romania. But someone told the family of a woman who knew how to perform abortions, although she was not medically trained, and would do it secretly. Magdalena reluctantly allowed a friend to take her to this woman to have the deed done. She knew she could go to prison for having an abortion. In letting the baby be killed, she might even die herself.

On the table, during the procedure, she lost a lot of blood and fainted. The unskilled abortionist became frightened and ran away for fear she would go to prison if caught. Magdalena's friend came into the room and took her to a hospital and to a doctor who knew the family. Learning that no one in the extended family wanted the child, and that Magdalena had agreed to an abortion to keep peace, he agreed to do it in spite of his fear of what might happen if anyone found out. He tried different procedures, including shots, to make the baby come.

After two days in the hospital, Magdalena became very weak. Finally, the doctor said to her, "This baby will not die; it wants to live." But because he did not know what the abortionist had done, he told her the baby might be physically handicapped, with no fingers or toes or possibly missing an arm or leg, and it might be mentally retarded.

The family decided to keep the baby.

A faithful member of the Orthodox Church, Magdalena believed in God. She made a covenant with God that if he let the baby be born healthy, she would give the child back to him to use in any way he chose. The tiny girl, born a month prematurely and weighing little more than four pounds, was kept in an incubator for two weeks. But as she grew, she was obviously quite normal.

The child was loved and treated specially. After some time, Magdalena sat down with her daughter and told her of the circumstances surrounding her birth. The girl is now twenty years old.

Magdalena had named her little girl Paula. I am that Paula. Magdalena is my mother. I am now a student preparing for a life of Christian service. It is not easy being in a different country, far away from those I love. But in my mother's womb, I refused to die. Today, I refuse to become anything other than the gift my mother promised to give back to God.

— As told to Rob L. Staples

Paula Ciniwass is a student at European Nazarene College (EUNC) in Busingen, a German enclave within Switzerland. Rob L. Staples is a professor of theology emeritus at Nazarene Theological Seminary in Kansas City. He interviewed Paula while serving as interim professor at EUNC during the fall of 2002.

Acknowledgements

Many thanks to all the "survivors" who shared their inspiring stories of faith, hope, and perseverance with us; to the staff and associates of Ascension Press for all their assistance in making yet another inspirational *Amazing Grace* book a reality.

– Jeff Cavins, Matthew Pinto, Patti Maguire Armstrong, and Luke Armstrong

Editor and Contributor Contact Information

To contact one of the contributors, please send correspondence the following address:

> *(Name of writer)*
> c/o Ascension Press
> P.O. Box 1990
> West Chester, PA 19380
> Or e-mail: info@ascensionpress.com

To contact one of the editors, please write them at one of the following addresses:

> Jeff Cavins
> P.O. Box 1533
> Maple Grove, MN 55311
> Or e-mail: jcavins@mac.com

> Matthew Pinto
> P.O. Box 1990
> West Chester, PA 19380
> Or e-mail: mpinto@ascensionpress.com

> Patti Maguire Armstrong, Luke Armstrong
> P.O. Box 1532
> Bismarck, ND 58502
> Or e-mail: patti@bis.midco.net (Patti) or
> lukespartacus@gmail.com (Luke)

About the Editors

Jeff Cavins served as a Protestant minister for twelve years before returning to the Catholic faith. His story is chronicled in his autobiography, *My Life on the Rock* (Ascension Press). Jeff is best-known as the founding host of the popular EWTN television program *Life on the Rock*. With Matthew Pinto, he is the co-creator of the *Amazing Grace* series, and is the author of *I'm Not Being Fed: Discovering the Food that Satisfies the Soul* (Ascension, 2005). Jeff is also the creator and principal author of *The Great Adventure*, a popular Bible study program. He and his wife, Emily, reside in Minnesota with their three daughters.

Matthew Pinto is the author of the best-selling question-and-answer book *Did Adam & Eve Have Belly Buttons?* (Ascension, 1998), co-author of *Did Jesus Have a Last Name?* (Ascension, 2005), and co-author of *A Guide to the Passion* (Ascension/ Catholic Exchange, 2004). Matt is co-founder of several Catholic organizations, including CatholicExchange.com, *Envoy* magazine, and the Theology of the Body Institute. He is the creator, with Jeff Cavins, of the *Amazing Grace* series. Matt and his wife, Maryanne, live in Pennsylvania with their five sons.

Patti Maguire Armstrong worked in the fields of social work and public administration before staying home full-time to raise her children. As a freelance writer, Patti has written more than 400 articles for both secular and religious publications. She has authored the book *Catholic Truths for Our Children* (www.raisingcatholickids.com) as a guide to help parents pass on the Catholic faith to their children and served as co-editor of four *Amazing Grace* books. Patti and her husband, Mark, live in North Dakota with their ten children.

Luke Armstrong is a graduate of North Dakota State University, with a double major in philosophy and English and a minor in Spanish. After spending his final semester studying in Valparaíso, Chile, he spent four months traveling through Central and South America. He is currently living in Antigua, Guatemala, where he is the program director for the charity Nuestros Ahijados as part of the God's Child Project (www.godschild.com). Luke is also a freelance writer currently looking to publish his first novel, *Leaving Left Behind*.